Deep Space

LIQUIFER — Living Beyond Earth
Architecture for
Extreme Environments

Mars

Moon

Orbit

Earth Land
Earth Ocean

PARK BOOKS

LIQUIFER

People can see the world as the room that they're in, or the street that they live on, or the town or city that they're in. Or, they can be aware—all the time—that we are all on a planet that's spinning on its own axis and orbiting the sun. So while we are all in our rooms, we are also ultimately part of a much much bigger structure, something bigger than all of us. We choose to see our place in the universe.

Niamh Shaw, STEM communicator, scientist, engineer, writer and performer
(Space Specials: Dream big or how to launch a career into space, 15 Dec 2020)

LIQUIFER Living Beyond Earth
Architecture for
Extreme Environments

PARK BOOKS

LIQUIFER

LIQUIFER   Living Beyond Earth
            Architecture for
            Extreme Environments

LIQUIFER

Table of Contents

Residing Among the Stars — 9
Prologue by Brent Sherwood

Living Beyond Earth — 15
Introduction by LIQUIFER

**Designing for Outer Space:
An Extreme Environment** — 40
Mars — 47

The Pursuit of Adaptability — 80
The Moon — 85

The New Vernacular in Outer Space — 106
Orbit — 113

When the Natural State is Motion — 131
Replicating Terrestrial Systems — 135
Earth: On Land — 141

**Mission Preparation:
Simulating Future Explorations** — 175
Earth: Underwater — 183

The Space–Earth Continuum — 204
Epilogue by Christina Ciardullo

Timeline of work — 208
Acronyms — 212
References — 213
Team Biographies — 218
Credits — 220
Colophon — 221

Table of Contents   The Projects

23   Travelling through the Extraterrestrial
     Conversation between the LIQUIFER team

     Mars Projects
52   SHEE — Self-Deployable Habitat for Extreme Environments
64   Moonwalk — Astronaut-Robot Cooperation on Mars
70   LavaHive — 3D Printed Martian Base
74   FASTER — Forward Acquisition of Soil and Terrain for
     Exploration Rover

     Moon Projects
90   RegoLight — Sintering Regolith with Solar Light
98   RAMA — Rover for Advanced Mission Applications
102 Smartie — Smart Resource Management
     based on Internet of Things

     Orbital Projects
118 Gateway I-Hab — International Habitat Module of the Lunar
     Gateway station
124 Deployable Getaway — Collapsible Crew Quarter
126 ISS-Sleep Kit — Sleeping in Space

     Earth Projects on Land
146 Eden-ISS — Plant Cultivation in Space
156 GrAB — Growing As Building
166 Living Architecture — Metabolic Apps
     for Programmable Buildings

     Earth Projects Underwater
188 Moonwalk — Astronaut-Robot Cooperation Underwater
194 Medusa — Underwater Research Habitat

     Expeditions
198 Antarctic Biennale — Planetary Systems Test-Bed
200 Deep Sea Minding — Thinking from the Ocean

Deep Space

Mars

Moon

Orbit

Earth Land
Earth Ocean

Residing Among the Stars

Prologue by
Brent Sherwood

Our past and future both reside among the stars.

Every atom in our bodies heavier than hydrogen—oxygen, carbon, nitrogen, phosphorus, sulphur and trace elements—was made in supernovae explosions more than five billion years ago.

We inhabit but an instant of time, a mere blink in the age of the universe. Our solar system is about one-third as old as the cosmos. Anatomically modern humans have roamed the Earth for less than 0.005 percent of its age, just 200,000 years. And human civilization—artefacts, writing, agriculture, technology, architecture and urbanism—has existed for only 5 percent of that brief time.

In just the last 200 years, a blip of the blink, humankind invented powered machinery, tamed electricity and fission, developed semiconductors and created the digital world. In so doing, we also reproduced to over eight billion people, consumed a third of our planet's forests, and overran the carrying capacity of the only biosphere we have. We are directly causing the planet's sixth large-scale extinction event. While the Earth is vast, an incomprehensible 6×10^{21} metric tons, our onion-skin-thin biosphere is not. The zone in which complex life can survive is quite limited and vulnerable, a fact that becomes more evident and inescapable every year. To coexist with the plummeting biodiversity remaining on Spaceship Earth, let alone to continue expanding indefinitely, we must return to space.

Only there will we find limitless energy, inexhaustible material resources and the opportunity to make new habitats so that human civilization and Earth life can have an unlimited future.

This existential opportunity should motivate all of us to open and settle the vast domain of space.

But living and thriving in space will be extremely different from what we know, because space is an extreme environment, everywhere. On the Moon, among the asteroids, on Mars, in free-space orbital habitats and eventually crossing interstellar distances, all the future places we could call home are soberingly and frustratingly hazardous and alien, and we must manufacture every aspect of our surroundings just to survive.

This is what Space Architecture is all about: "the theory and practice of designing and building inhabited environments for use in outer space". Space Architecture's built environments must be tailored for the diverse harsh conditions found in terrestrial analogue extreme environments, in Earth orbit, on the Moon, asteroids, Mars and in deep space.

What began as a visionary urge shared by a few curious, future-oriented designers in the late 20th century has become a new professional field of thought and endeavour. Increasingly, Space Architecture appears relevant to our predicament on this limited Earth by offering practical, incremental solutions. The outward-looking solutions aim to tame the harsh domain of space to enable a long tomorrow; the inward-looking solutions aim to transfer lessons from space flight directly back to Earth today, informing a lighter touch on our unique, irreplaceable home.

This book chronicles the journey of an intrepid team of explorers. LIQUIFER comprises a flexible team of designers who are committed to advancing human space flight by designing what it could be, while also making it quintessentially humanistic and promoting our noblest goals: safety, practicality, comfort, productivity, frugality, ingenuity and inspiration. LIQUIFER has, for decades, pioneered the special role of Space Architecture within large aerospace teams, using their ingenuity and humanistic system design principles to earn a seat at the table alongside government agencies and industry leaders.

Living Beyond Earth: Architecture for Extreme Environments contains mind-expanding designs for some of the extreme environments of outer space where gravity becomes a parameter, life support systems must work continuously and reliably, and transformable and lightweight designs make solutions possible. Throughout LIQUIFER's approach, nature and humanity remain fundamental.

Along this journey, you will be invited to contemplate deeply challenging questions that percolate at the core of the new field of Space Architecture: <u>What is it about space that seems to pull us outward inexorably?</u> Maybe it's the infinite view. On Earth our horizon is limited by topography and atmospheric haze, while beneath the sea, light scattering and attenuation close us in. But in space we can see forever, all the way back to the origin of the universe. How could this not compel us to explore and expand?
<u>What motivates Space Architects?</u> The allure of designing places for human activity in novel conditions, where even gravity and breath cannot be taken for granted, is so fundamental to the act of architecture that it has become a siren song for many. Architects love hard design problems, which are puzzles of form, material and building. What greater challenge could there be than taming space to make an infinite future for humanity?

<u>What by nature do we require?</u> The rigours of space separate wants from needs. What is atavistic—so intrinsic to human nature and social behaviour that it cannot be changed? Which needs aren't actually needs at all, but merely habits from living on Earth? <u>What if Lunar or Mars partial gravity isn't physiologically tolerable forever?</u> We will need to learn what our deep needs are and accommodate them wherever we find ourselves. Finally, "designer biology" is advancing rapidly; will space humans even be the same as us?

<u>How will we adapt to inconceivably big numbers?</u> Space is truly vast. Travel distances are measured in millions of kilometres and months of time. Even the speed of light becomes noticeable: from Earth, 1.3 seconds to the Moon and nine minutes to the stable Sun-Earth Lagrange Points. Real-time conversations will be impossible between dispersed space habitats. How will we make the transition from our finite Earth to infinite space that still imposes finite constraints? Eventual space urbanism will be different from today's megacities. "Towns" will be modest in scale and months or years apart, as they used to be on Earth.

<u>Can human behaviour evolve?</u> We want to believe that civilization can make the social animal more responsible but history's evidence is not heartening. Will the privation we experience in space cause us to learn new ways of being or will we just extend old habits with us everywhere we go? Can luxury be compatible with draconian efficiency and extreme physical conservation? Increasingly, architecture has enabled social density but arguably it has not really improved human behaviour. Will things be different in space? Will harsh conditions drive spiritual growth?

<u>What about architecture is essential to human community?</u> In space we will learn how technology and community size relate to remote self-sufficiency. Can we learn to consume without appropriating or even use without consuming? Who determines acceptable risk in reaching out a great distance and who gets to go? Utopian and dystopian futures are in tension throughout speculative fiction and in today's world. Will expanding into space be ennobling or oppressive?

This book touches the deep questions that Space Architects engage, argue about and hold in mind as they work. Immersed in LIQUIFER's forward-thinking Space Architecture projects, your imagination will ultimately leave you pondering what types of society we will build in space.

Deep Space

Mars

Moon

Orbit

Earth Land
Earth Ocean

Living Beyond Earth

Introduction by LIQUIFER

An interstellar traveller aiming to land on Earth's surface will first encounter a dense, spherical skin of satellites. Approaching Earth through the floating infrastructural haze of the exosphere, the size and shape of one of these satellites will make it stand out. Large panels catching sunlight cover a series of modules and a docking spaceship. It is a space station, home to a handful of humans, orbiting at a distance of 400 kilometres from the planetary surface where each and every other living human resides, along with millions more species.

The International Space Station (ISS) is a technological biosphere in which we explore what it takes to make a new home beyond our planet, now joined in Earth's orbit by China's Tiangong. Constructing such specialised architecture for the extreme environment of space is an endeavour with few parallels in either its complexity or the ingenuity required for success. Its architects are tasked with fulfilling the basic needs of human survival and, at the same time, allowing a small community to live in harmony, far from the familiar, terrestrial environment with which we have co-evolved. This is the challenge LIQUIFER has been engaging for the last 20 years.

This book is built upon the insight gained from this living laboratory and looks towards the far greater settlements we will build, much further from home. Our work at LIQUIFER spans the space-Earth continuum, learning from the constraints imposed by outer space to provide for humans on Earth, in addition to those few who are venturing beyond. From our perspective Earth is one part of space and space is all around us.

The space–Earth continuum

Our endeavours share one goal, whether delivering humankind beyond the universe's unknown frontiers or finding strategies for more sustainable living on Earth: to support life and to advance knowledge through the combined efforts of science, technology and architecture. Human beings share the same physical needs whether they are astronauts living on a space station or the inhabitants of a house on Earth. Shelter, water, food and oxygen are the essentials for survival. In extreme environments, where the conditions are unforgiving, humans are driven to manage these resources with utmost care.

Architecture goes beyond the provision of essentials for human survival. Manufacturing a technological biosphere for living beyond Earth also requires the design of a quality living environment and a space for thriving social systems. Extreme environments demand invention, adaptation and dedication from those who design them and those who live in them.

Collaboration as a mindset

The expansion of human presence beyond Earth's horizon is driven by collective imagination, which has already mobilised global networks of resources and ingenuity. The collaborative efforts of teams with diverse sets of knowledge and skills enable the complex solutions required for human space exploration. By setting our practice's default attitude to Space Architecture as firmly transdisciplinary, we ensure diverse perspectives and approaches guide the future outcomes of life in outer space.

LIQUIFER has evolved with direction from its core team of Barbara Imhof, Waltraut Hoheneder and René Waclavicek. Beginning in 2003 with expertise in architecture, design, space applications and economics, the team has since expanded to include systems designers, material scientists, aeronautical engineers and engineering technicians. Our work is predominantly collaborative and routinely part of an international consortium made up of leading industries and academia. These partnerships are financed by the European Union, European Space Agency (ESA), Austrian Research Promotion Agency (FFG), and the Austrian Science Fund (FWF). As a micro-enterprise embedded in cutting-edge science and technology developments for human spaceflight, we develop concepts, scenarios, prototypes, systems and products for future living and working on Earth and in space.

The history of a name

In the late 1990s, the Australian geologist Nick Hoffman established the "White Mars" hypothesis. He challenged the common assumption that the valley networks on the Martian surface were formed by water, suggesting they could have been shaped by other media. The White Mars hypothesis posited that carbon dioxide flows determined Martian surface features, generating liquifers, not aquifers. In the early noughties, this theory was disproved but it can still encourage thinking beyond the paradigm of Earth. The name LIQUIFER holds this ambition to broaden the range of perspectives, to challenge conventions and investigate the full range of alternative solutions.

A journey through space

LIQUIFER Living Beyond Earth: Architecture for Extreme Environments maps a journey from outer space to our own planet. Our projects are contextualised in the profoundly diverse environments found along the way. LIQUIFER's architectural design concepts, feasibility studies and technological developments confront scarcity issues that challenge life on Mars, the Moon, in Orbit and on Earth.

Woven through this planetary backdrop, a series of texts elaborate the parameters that drive design for outer space, including the utilisation of in-situ resources, the integration of life-support systems, and the requirement to respond to diverse gravitational conditions.

There are multiple routes to navigate this book. For multi-directional travel, the key concepts and projects are connected through a series of wormholes, which can transport you, for example, to the Moon → p. 85 or Mars → p. 47. For a location-based, condition-specific reading of our work, one must ascend or descend through the structure of the book. For a chronological understanding, a timeline → p. 209 documenting our full portfolio is available at the back of the book.

LIQUIFER's work is framed by essays from acclaimed Space Architects Brent Sherwood and Christina Ciardullo. Looking at our work with their own experience, both authors expand on what it takes to be a Space Architect and what it means to envisage how humans may live in outer space in the future. To begin the book, we introduce our team with a series of conversations revealing personal views, ambitions and visions for the future of human life here and beyond Earth.

Join us in our journey from outer space: we will land on the windblown surfaces of Mars, in the silent craters of the Moon, and float through the microgravity of orbital stations, before returning to our home planet.

Deep Space

Mars

Moon

Orbit

Earth Land
Earth Ocean

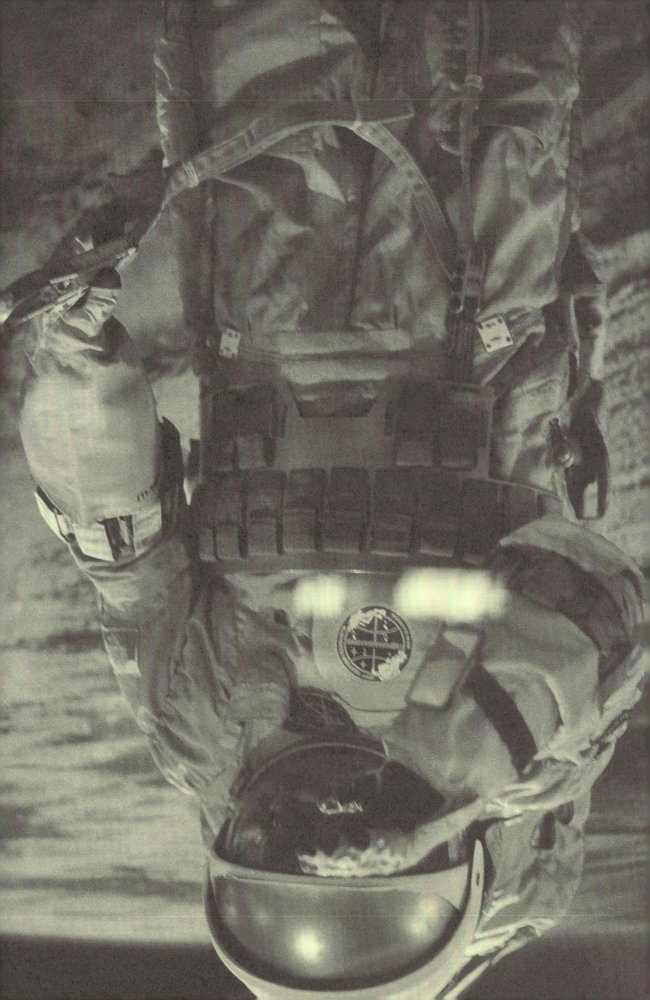

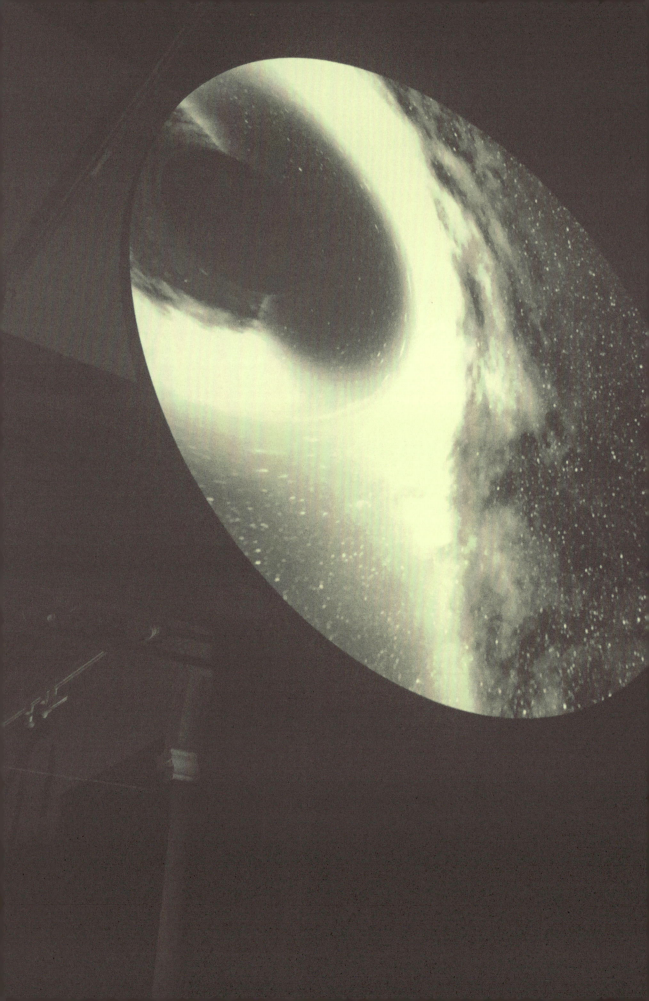

Travelling through the Extraterrestrial

Space Architects are asked one question repeatedly: why put all your effort into outer space when there are so many things to be fixed on Earth? The simple reality is that many people dream of space. As Eva Diáz wrote, outer space is "the place wherein reside fantasies of rebirth, of reinvention, of escape from historical determinations of class, race, and gender inequality, and of aspirations for just societies beyond the protection of the Earth's atmosphere."[1]

We at LIQUIFER each decided to be part of the mission to shape these other worlds. Connected by our passion for outer space, the team pursues a familiar dream, motivated by the complex challenges that arise throughout this extreme environment. Our work is realised due to the variety of opinions, values and voices we bring to the table. In the following series of conversations, we speculate, dream and discuss past, present and future engagements with space. Just like sharing opinions over lunch in our Vienna office, these conversations felt like the most natural way to present the team, our exchange of ideas and how the practice has formed. The conversations invite the reader to reflect on the individual viewpoints of the team, what motivates us to explore outer space, the possibilities in future human spaceflight, the perspective of the architect in outer space, the impact of policy on our work and how knowledge developed for space returns to Earth.

Susmita Mohanty Asking why humans go to space is a bit like asking why people desire to climb the Himalayas—because it is there. It is often human nature to seek out the unknown or find a way to get to the unreachable.

Bob Davenport After 50 years in this business, I think the real motivation to go to space is simply that we want to do it. We want to be present as human beings in outer space. We want to do the exploration ourselves, whatever that exploration is. We are motivated by challenges. And I think that these extreme environments provide many people with super challenges.

Chris Gilbert Agreed. In other words, it's a measure of our achievements.

Stephen Ransom My interest developed during the time I was designing complex planetary surface habitats and vehicles and launch systems to fulfil international requirements. It also opened up the need for extensive historical research to understand the problems engineers faced in previous space programmes and the solutions they found to fulfil particular applications. Both stressed the need to build teams to combine their experience and expertise.

René Waclavicek For me, the unknown sparks curiosity and establishes my drive and motivation. There are still so many unanswered questions. Are we the only intelligent lifeform in the universe? Has there ever been life on Mars? Will we establish a base on the Moon? As children we ask questions to get a better understanding of our world. Venturing into space with robots and humans replaces old questions with new ones. By advancing into space, our horizon expands.

Waltraut Hoheneder I agree, asking questions is inherent to human life. Human space flight is part of basic research on the fundamentals of human existence—on medical, psychological and environmental issues that are necessary to sustain and promote human life. It is about understanding the prerequisites of human life to not only survive but thrive, even under extreme conditions.

Barbara Imhof   I think the question of why we explore also needs to be framed in a suitable manner. We can use narratives for our motivation that talk about our questions and the answers we have already found. The narrative of the Space Race in the 1960s inspired a whole generation, produced countless scientific publications and many innovations in material science and computer technology. The activities around this race also found a memorable place in our global culture. With narratives we can contextualise our motivation and allow it to be remembered.

Susmita Mohanty   We are increasingly confronted with a narrative that Earth might become uninhabitable for humans.

Waltraut Hoheneder   I deeply question the scenario that human space exploration is important because Earth might not be inhabitable anymore. Who would leave the planet and what about the others? This is not a vision I share, rather I think that we will combine all our efforts into restoring the environment on Earth.

Daniel Schubert   I always say to my students we are already astronauts living on a foreign planet. Earth is a testbed for ecological living and we can transfer that knowledge to the Moon or Mars. By creating biospheres and closed-loop systems we will learn how to leave this planet alone.

Monika Brandić Lipińska   I would like to do something that would allow us to avoid the question of why we should go to space when we have to solve the problems on Earth. It would be great to maintain the narrative that space exploration really helps Earth because Earth is also one of the planets in space. It's not that because we have to solve problems on Earth, we shouldn't think about space. Instead, thinking about Earth and thinking about outer space need to be understood as the same line of thought.

René Waclavicek   The narrative is that everything is interconnected. Earth is part of space and space is all around us.

Life in Deep Space

When we think about the future, we have the tendency to consider it a blank page. Ramia Mazé challenges this thinking in a 2017 essay entitled 'Design and the Future: Temporal Politics of "Making a Difference"', writing: "The future is by no means empty, it will be occupied by built environments, infrastructures, and things that we have designed, it will bear the consequences of our history, structures, policies, and lifestyles, which we daily reproduce by habit or with intent and design."[2]
The material futures for life in Deep Space however appear more blank, leaving room for different approaches to the challenge of sustaining life in such extreme environments.

Daniel Schubert   There is an interesting development within exoplanet research that's going on right now. Virtually every day they are finding a new "Earth" somewhere in the Milky Way. Technologies will continue to advance. It is likely that they will find another civilization outside the solar system.

Monika Brandić Lipińska   Our thinking about the future of space exploration might drastically change after we find life. It's hard to predict how much impact it will have on our life here, the insight that we're not the only ones. How would this impact our central beliefs? What would it mean for religion?

Susmita Mohanty   Humans are always looking for carbon-based life forms. In Avi Loeb's recent book, he says we need to look for industrial signatures.[3] Currently, we are obsessed with this whole carbon-based economy, but we need to broaden our search. Let's say, in the past, a certain planet might have had an industrial civilization. So, are there any remnants of that technological past?

Monika Brandić Lipińska   That reminds me of a conversation with Jill Tarter, co-founder of the SETI Institute,[4] and the American journalist Krista Tippett on what kind of life is going to be found first: will it be biological or technology-based life?[5] There are so many ideas of how to find technology. We are only looking for life as we know it, carbon-based life, and there may be so many other life forms that we cannot even imagine out there. We are looking at everything from our own perspective. The perspective may completely change in 1,000 years.

René Waclavicek   There may be lifeforms based on elements other than carbon. However, due to its structural properties, the number of possible combinations carbon can build is by far greater than the number of chemical compounds of all other elements combined. So, it doesn't seem far-fetched to assume that a significant number of alien lifeforms out there might be made-up of carbon-based chemical compounds. When we look at how long life on Earth was dominated by microbes before a civilisation developed that could leave traces of technological development, we can assume that most traces of life we may find out there are microbial. Of course, we shouldn't limit our search to microbes. Since 1984 the SETI Institute has been searching for signals from extraterrestrial intelligence. This research is pursued regardless of chemical composition. Of course, we can also search for remnants of civilisations but in a galactic timescale they might vanish very fast. They may therefore be even harder to find than active civilisations emitting detectable signals.

Waltraut Hoheneder   In work we are inclined to speak about settlements and not colonisation in order to think about bases on the Moon and on Mars from a non-violent perspective. A lot of our projects deal with very careful use of local resources. We have a duty of care for these resources and to any kind of extraterrestrial lifeform we might encounter. We cannot afford to make the same mistakes we made on Earth, so we ensure our approach differs from the extractivist principles that currently guide many economies on Earth.

Susmita Mohanty   Just imagine we go to Mars and find native extremophiles and tell them: "Hey, look, we discovered you! Next, we shall document you. Take you to Earth, maybe. Even own you. Monetise the hell out of you." And make a fool of ourselves, all over again, as we did on our home planet. We are very good at that sort of thing.

Barbara Imhof   What I find quite interesting is that we are currently looking at habitable planets, which are very far away in a distant solar system, light years away. When we talk about space exploration nowadays, we mostly talk about dimensions and kilometres; let's say, we need to travel 400 million kilometres to get to Mars or 350,000 kilometres to the Moon. But we have no grasp of light years and we are very far away from being able to travel that far and that fast. In the end, I think humans will always be stuck around Earth, unless we actually start to build generation spaceships. Then we could venture out and go further. When humans are able to do this, there will be a population that leaves Earth and probably never comes back.

Susmita Mohanty   I'd like to sign up for a hibernation experiment. I'd like to hibernate my way to a faraway galaxy. It'd be nice to leave and go on a long voyage to an unknown place with a bunch of like-minded friends. We could start experimenting by sleeping our way to our next-door neighbour Mars. For that, the voyagers would have to be induced into hibernation using drugs and put inside small individual soft-shell pods—like the ones you find in the Clarke-Kubrick science-fiction film. The pods would be darkened and cooled to keep the bodies of the space voyagers at a low temperature for most of the 180-day journey from Earth to Mars.[6]

René Waclavicek   Konstantin Tsiolkovsky wrote that "Earth is the cradle of humanity, but one cannot live in a cradle forever."[7] If Earth is our cradle, the Solar System is our nursery. Human Mars exploration is a necessary stepping stone in learning how to step out of our cradle and learn to walk as an interplanetary and—maybe one day— an interstellar species.

Susmita Mohanty   To me, the prospect of interplanetary travel is like intercontinental travel. It is a matter of overcoming distances through advances in science and technology, as well as the necessary adaptation of human physiology, sociology and psychology for these new journeys.

Monika Brandić Lipińska   If I were born on Mars or somewhere else, I would need a spacesuit to go to Earth, to visit my ancestral origin. Due to growing up in these different environments, a specific architecture might be necessary, like a hotel for people coming from other planets.

Barbara Imhof   That reminds me of '3001', the science-fiction book by Arthur C. Clarke.[8] The protagonist cannot return to Earth completely because his physiology wouldn't allow him to be exposed to terrestrial gravity. A friend takes the space elevator into the Earth's Orbit to visit him in microgravity where he hovers in Orbit.

René Waclavicek   We are witnessing a process similar to when life on Earth left the oceans. Living organisms advanced into regions not inhabitable at that time, preparing the ground for what is an integral part of our biosphere today. Life adapted to new environmental conditions, instead of trying to turn land into ocean.

Waltraut Hoheneder   Technological and living systems will merge. They are merging already in many applications. Technological parts are implanted in living organisms as part of medical treatment: artificial joints, metal plates, tissues—some of them of other organic origin. In the future, technological and biological systems might merge to an extent that their origins are hardly traceable. Advances in artificial intelligence, deep learning and directed evolution may generate life forms, agents and actors, where the distinction between artificial and natural, between technological and biological, become irrelevant.

Susmita Mohanty   If we can start replacing joints and organs with new ones, reverse or prevent osteoporosis, correct age-related diseases propagated through genes and so on, we can certainly extend human lifespans. Maybe in the future we can live for 120 years, 150 years or longer? I think medical advances will allow that. How, then, are we going to accommodate the ever-increasing ageing population?

Barbara Imhof   I read a book by Richard Morgan called *Altered Carbon*, it is about the brain and body being separated yet contained in one physical element.[9] In Morgan's scenario, the brain—or what constitutes us as a thinking species—can be stored as a collection of data in a so-called stack. The body is added to the physical presence as a suit or sleeve. Together, this results in a human being who can potentially live forever, since everything can either be stored as a stack or uploaded into any sleeve. In this world people don't travel with their bodies. They just send their mind as digital information at light speed to their destination, where it is uploaded to another sleeve. Such a scenario is interesting for space exploration because it could enable our species to travel immense distances and act independently in those far-off environments. The field of "Artificial Life" is aiming in a similar direction already. In the deep future, the scenario described above could perhaps be a reality in one way or another. Human space exploration might be able to overcome great distances and time through methods of compacting the self.

Space Architecture

Buckminster Fuller's famous quote "We are all astronauts" not only frames Earth as a spaceship but also suggests that all architects are Space Architects.[10]

Monika Brandić Lipińska   We currently separate the architecture on the Moon or Mars, or asteroids and so on, from architecture on Earth. Further in the future, architecture on Earth will also be considered space architecture.

Daniel Schubert   Some science-fiction movies might begin to look like documentaries.

Chris Gilbert   We have been fed a diet of science-fiction stories and future scenarios for so long that we are taking it for granted that we will live on the Moon and on Mars. It is so easy to create convincing science fiction-based films, with luxurious spaceships appearing to fly at many times the speed of light, but we don't really spend enough time trying to understand or analyse what it will take to achieve these future scenarios. So it is becoming easier to promote visions of settlements in space without giving due consideration to the technological hurdles that must be overcome.

Daniel Schubert   To build a habitat on Mars or the Moon, I think there will be five main functions that every human habitat needs to fulfil. The first function is "In-Situ Resource Utilisation": → p. 106 utilising the resources that can be found there (water, oxygen, fuel, energy, consumables). The second function is "Recycling": in order to establish a closed-loop system in which all the precious resources that have been generated by resource utilisation will be recycled, together with the goods that are transported from Earth. There will be physical and chemical systems, biological systems, recycling of air, water and non-bio-consumables such as plastics and metal, and so on. The third function is "Build and Repair": if something breaks within a habitat, you have to go and repair it, you have to be able to produce spare parts on your own, → p. 102 and, if you have one habitat nucleus, you might want to build a new habitat somewhere else. This function will enable you to reproduce the complete habitat. And since it is a small system—an ecosystem, a biosphere, an ecosphere, or whatever you want to call it—with a lot of players such as humans, machines, animals, plants, you need to "Balance and Control" it, which is the fourth function. You have to be careful that something is not overshooting that could destabilise the whole ecosystem or eventually the whole society. This is something we have not done here on Earth. We are just starting by shifting from fossil energy to renewable energy, for example. In a very small habitat system, you have to balance and control because the buffers are very small. You see imbalances immediately and they might have devastating effects. That's why you have to keep an eye on them. Lastly, the fifth function is "Resilience and Wellbeing". There will be humans who live in those early habitats. They need to survive and be healthy. It does not make sense to build a big structure, and then nobody wants to live there, or goes there and unfortunately dies after two years. So, apart from system resilience, human factors play an important role which includes telemedicine or medicine in general. I consider those five key functions mandatory for a future habitat on the Moon and Mars. And if you miss out on one, you will fail.

Monika Brandić Lipińska   I think, quite soon, all these visionary ideas for space architecture such as In-Situ Resource Utilisation, → p. 106 will be applied, pushed further by current research and development in experimental architecture. Using the local resources on the Moon and on Mars yields a lot of potential for extracting water and other resources and using 3D printing technologies → p. 90 to construct safe habitats for humans to live in.

René Waclavicek   Some major technical challenges need to be mastered. Developing an autonomous robotic construction process is one, finding solutions for radiation protection is another. These will strongly depend on the funding of research in Lunar exploration.

Stephen Ransom   Long-duration human and robotic exploration of the Moon and Mars will require mobility, in-situ resources and radiation protection. For the Moon and Mars, mobile pressurised manned habitats and laboratories with refuelling capabilities, which have propellants derived from local surface minerals and atmospheric gases, will be needed. New forms of surface manoeuvrability, such as small single-wheeled vehicles, could offer other types of exploration or construction opportunities. These could be operated as clusters where planets have relatively dense atmospheres (e.g. Mars and Titan). Balloons, dirigible airships, fixed-wing aircraft, helicopters, autogyros or even flapping-wing ornithopters might find applications on sites remote from the landing area.

Barbara Imhof   Humans are living beings whose functionality and physiology require gravity. That is our evolutionary development. Our bodies require us to build space stations that rotate and therefore create artificial gravity. There we could live almost as we do on Earth. These wheel-shaped space stations were first conceived by Konstantin Tsiolkovsky before further development by Herman Potočnik, detailing by Wernher von Braun and finally scenic realisations by von Braun and Walt Disney. *2001: A Space Odyssey* by Stanley Kubrick and Arthur C. Clarke is a wonderful illustration of such a construction and I think this is also the future of the long-term habitation for many people beyond the Earth's horizon, without causing too much damage or disruption to their health.[11] Of course, this also requires appropriate radiation protection.

René Waclavicek   There may be a time in which the Earth's Orbit has transformed into a living zone, extending the Earth's boundary. I can imagine that there could be an infrastructure ring around the Earth (in Orbit) that is inhabited by many of us and is a self-sufficient ecosphere partly in zero gravity and partly in artificial gravity. It would be a belt of orbital platforms that serve as the extension of our cradle and at the same time as a starting point, a harbour to access further destinations through shuttle services to the Moon, Mars and asteroids.

Waltraut Hoheneder   A big issue with living in space will be how to compensate for the radical reduction in the number and variety of stimuli that humans are usually exposed to in terrestrial environments. Human life is characterised by rhythms that build on change, alternating periods of extroversion and introversion, of meeting and retreating, of going out and coming home. A lively travel activity between space and Earth might be feasible within low Earth orbit →p.113 but how would this work when venturing into deep space?

Daniel Schubert My motivation when working in space is the creation of closed-loop systems, eco-spheres, biospheres. What I want to see is that we will have some sort of closed-loop habitat on the Moon and that we know so much about habitats and biospheres that we understand how to live independent from resupply.

René Waclavicek Yes, the Moon →p. 85 will teach us how to establish permanent outposts under similar conditions. The Moon is the testbed for Mars. Some say that the first Mars →p.47 astronaut is already born. Today we are searching for ways to take necessary parts of our biosphere with us in our spacecraft. We are working on solutions to become independent from Earth to try to survive in the hostile environment of outer space.

Waltraut Hoheneder We have been working on projects that envision self-organising building systems, which may eventually be able to take full care of the needs of their inhabitants. Human space flight might sooner or later be able to get very close to this vision, creating supportive and reliable habitats that host space travellers, to create habitats with adaptable life support systems →p.135 aligned with the travellers' needs. The habitats could have their own identities and thrive on their own, in the same way that living organisms do on Earth. Microbes could be the main lifeform supporting these habitable systems. With their self-regulating capacities, microbes might be indispensable for the smooth operation of any infrastructure whether on the Moon, Mars or Earth, →p.141 and especially during deep-space missions.

Space Policies

The governments of major world powers and their outlook on space exploration continue to be the greatest factor affecting funding opportunities for space development. However, the growth of commercial NewSpace →p. 212 companies will impact how space is experienced and who is able to experience it. Importantly, and realistically, whether humans will one day find themselves on the surface of Mars, orbiting the Moon or on a journey deeper into space will also depend upon unfolding events on Earth—be they the result of political, economical or environmental change.

Bob Davenport Tourism is the big thing at the moment. It will likely be the driver for commercial interest. I expect it is going to take off in the near future, in which case I think we might soon see the first hotel in space.

Chris Gilbert Yes, we can, I think, fairly safely predict the growth of commercial spaceflight in low Earth orbit and perhaps suborbital. Probably, if you can bring the cost down quickly, there are sufficient people willing to pay for a flight in space. That might help commercial spaceflight in the long term by stimulating demand for full space flights. The problem with encouraging commercial activities in space is the constant pressure to produce short-term returns on the investment. This leads, for example, to Earth-centric space already being seriously contaminated with debris.

Susmita Mohanty In the 21st Century, the space race is no longer between nations but between private companies.

Bob Davenport I would like to see a positive commercialisation of the low Earth orbit environment and not just commercialisation, but also the continued implementation of basic research, so that the International Space Station concept continues or comparable new facilities are built.

Monika Brandić Lipińska   Now we have people living on the ISS but they are not citizens of ISS. Whenever we go to the Moon, it will just be people from Earth going for a mission to the Moon. But when will there be a shift that means people will identify with the Moon or Mars? When will they try to establish their own time zones? Will they be able to begin from scratch?

René Waclavicek   How do we propose living together in a society in outer space? How large is that population?

Daniel Schubert   In the far future of 100 years plus, we might have space settlements, perhaps several thousand people on Mars, and then there might be a time when the Martians will say we want to be independent. Perhaps there will even be a war—who knows? Possibly in the next 500 years, there will be a Martian Independence War. And people on the Moon might also claim independence.

René Waclavicek   When I think of 100 years in the future, I have to look back 100 years to be able to imagine the options. Back then, we were speculating about space travel in a very fantastical way. The mobility age had just begun and with it came the dawn of our understanding and production of today's technologies. We were, so to speak, at a turning point of culture: experiencing the Suffragette movement in Europe, the slow (and continued) demise of colonialism, a shift from monarchies to democracies and other marked changes in political power.

Waltraut Hoheneder   It might be possible that people on Mars do not aspire towards independence. Autonomous living will be part of their everyday life. By then independence might not be even considered desirable, knowing that living systems generally depend on each other.

Susmita Mohanty   We need to introspect how human presence should be responsibly developed in outer space.

René Waclavicek   We should refer to the peaceful uses as stated within the Outer Space Treaty of 1967 in the future for establishing a society and defining common practices.¹² Specific Lunar cultural practices will form in settlements, first, as we see with the International Space Station, even if Lunar bases are distant from each other.

Monika Brandić Lipińska   We once had a team project on Lunar settlement development and we could approach it any way we wanted.¹³ So, we started to think of what we want to do, the time frame, where and what the settlement would be about. Then our discussions shifted from thinking about the space habitat and space settlement into the fact that we don't really have guidelines for how to develop Lunar settlements. With the United Nations Sustainability Goals in our mind, we developed 15 Lunar Sustainability Goals. We made our project based on UN goals but you cannot really map them directly onto space projects, so we developed a series of goals relevant to the environment and concerns of human settlement in space. We developed goals such as: open access, peaceful purposes, international cooperation, education and outreach, heritage protection, health and safety, transportation, zero waste, space debris mitigation, sustainable ISRU → p. 106 and so on.

Chris Gilbert   I wish that the spacefaring nations take more steps to make space travel sustainable, especially in near-Earth orbits, → p. 113 by passing effective legislation requiring satellite operators to remove existing debris when launching new satellites. Currently, new satellite constellations are being launched with inadequate accountability for long-term debris problems they may cause in the future.

Barbara Imhof   In-Situ Resource Utilisation → p. 106 is an important topic, to find resources locally within close proximity to extra-terrestrial settlements. When the infrastructure grows, resources further away from the base can be targeted. That is what humans did on Earth. If our future is a series of joint ventures between governmental, taxpayer-paid missions, and commercial stakeholders, then the question is: to whom do the resources belong? In the Outer Space Treaty there is a paragraph that says: "Outer space is not subject to national appropriation by claim of sovereignty, by means of use or occupation, or by any other means."¹⁴ The Artemis Accords, which [at the time of print] were recently signed by 24 countries and one territory, excludes this paragraph when they claim "extraction of space resources does not inherently constitute national appropriation."¹⁵ The legal aspect of space exploration needs to be defined in the coming years and we need to set a course for how we want to share and distribute resources.

René Waclavicek   Let's take Antarctica as an example. There are 1000 people overwintering but in summer the population increases to around 8000 researchers and 35000 tourists. That could be a valid scenario for the first settlements on the Moon as well. Although Antarctica is not a state and the governing rules depend on the bases' nationalities, there is a certain way of coexistence established amongst the researchers who overwinter. It is probably defined through personal bonds that form a specific culture from living in extreme environments. I assume that people in distress are supported by the closest bases regardless of nationality. I have heard that scientific findings are interchanged by scientists through personal communication rather than through their supporting agencies. The tourists belong to another group in that they enter the continent mainly or only via the Antarctic Peninsula and they are kept separate from the researchers to a large extent. However, all human activity is governed by the Antarctic Treaty of 1959 and connected to the Protocol on Environmental Protection to the Antarctic Treaty, which was established in 1991.¹⁶

Monika Brandić Lipińska   So Lunar or Martian bases could potentially work in a similar way to those in Antarctica where research and development is mainly funded by governments. Maybe it could also rely on money from public-private partnerships that would be given to research and science.

Daniel Schubert   In that sense, you could even see Antarctica as an analogue, not only as a testing ground but perhaps also for how to best settle on Mars. In the beginning there were expeditions; then there was the race for who would reach the South Pole first. Then in the early years of the last century, there were more and more small stations, occupied only for a couple of months, which in time became permanently inhabited.

Susmita Mohanty   We can start by treating the Moon as our eighth continent for purposes of legal and policy deliberation. Antarctica, our seventh continent, could serve as a precedent to ensure we do not destroy a shared resource despite vested interests and pressure to monetise. If we refuse to act, we will wreck the Moon, much the same way we have wrecked low Earth orbit with millions of human-made debris objects due to the absence of farsighted laws.

René Waclavicek   So, hundreds of years in the future, there might be an advanced society where environmental protection laws are established and where community and capital are hopefully more justly distributed.

Waltraut Hoheneder   Maybe the concept of capital and ownership will have been abandoned by then, not only because of the immense top-down administrative efforts involved but also with the overwhelming establishment of self-organising, open-source infrastructure. Then self-regulatory, robotic infrastructure, enhanced by living systems, will constitute the permanent settlements as independent legal identities. Humans—or whatever they might be called by then—might share a nomadic lifestyle and refrain from settling down.

Space Technologies for Earth

Due to climate change, the number of extreme environments on Earth is increasing. As a consequence, the challenges terrestrial architects face will become much more closely aligned with those of Space Architects.

Chris Gilbert I think there will be increased requirements that institutional space budgets should be spent on projects with viable benefits to terrestrial problems.

Susmita Mohanty There are studies that show that the Earth, as a planet, can only sustain about 2 billion people with the consumption patterns we see in the US. Many people consume way more than they need or way more than what they are willing to neutralise. I think that is the difference: we humans have completely lost a sense of balance and scale.

Waltraut Hoheneder Human space exploration requires long-term thinking, which is not necessarily characteristic of our common interpretation of evolution as being driven by reactive patterns that allow adaptation to changing environments. Global terrestrial challenges nowadays require long-term approaches as well, since it became obvious with the development of the atomic bomb and human-driven climate change that humans hold the potential to destroy the environment upon which they depend.

Bob Davenport Human space exploration and aspirations to mitigate terrestrial climate change focus on the same goal: to ensure liveable conditions for humans, by studying the underlying principles of healthy biospheres, and to apply the findings to support and generate them on multiple scales. Our motivations on Earth are comparable.

Waltraut Hoheneder I agree, human space flight is a testbed for exploring the nature of circularity that enables self-sustaining systems in smaller biospheres. These can generate insights that support the shift towards circular economies on planet Earth.

René Waclavicek New greenhouse concepts → p. 146 necessary for a closed-loop life support system → p. 135 for a permanent presence in space can help make terrestrial food production much more efficient, environmentally friendly and less ground-consuming.

Waltraut Hoheneder Humankind has developed technologies that happen to correspond to human or animal systems: they consume organic matter and oxygen, and generate carbon dioxide. In production processes here on Earth, → p. 141 we largely lack technologies that complement such processes, that enable circularity by generating oxygen and consuming carbon dioxide like that of photosynthesis in natural systems. Establishing artificial biospheres in outer space will require careful attention to balancing systems and the development of biotechnological innovations in order to close cycles which may supply important insights for a paradigm shift on Earth.

Daniel Schubert Mars or the Moon, these are our testbeds, and we can transfer the knowledge back to Earth. We should be able to be really self-sustaining. Once we understand how to do this then it doesn't matter where we live anymore— we could live on the Moon or on Mars or somewhere else in space, maybe near Jupiter, wherever. It doesn't matter because we would be a self-sustaining society living in our own closed-loop environment. We would be completely independent from terrestrial resources. We should aim, in the habitats we live in now, to limit or minimise our ecological footprint towards zero. We should already live today as if we were on a foreign planet.

Susmita Mohanty According to The Millennium Charter [a 2002 mission statement that articulated the fundamental principles of space architecture], "Space Architecture is the theory and practice of designing and building inhabited environments in outer space."[17,18] → p. 40 Many considerations familiar to Space Architects—productivity, privacy, assembly, aesthetics, identity, sensations, views, mood, safety, utilities and adaptive use, to name just a few—are increasingly relevant to the design of habitable environments in dense cities.[19] Living both in space and in dense cities brings into sharp focus considerations such as sustainability, material recycling and regenerative life support →p.166

Monika Brandić Lipińska   I think we should make it clear to the public and to people who are not necessarily interested in space exploration that the goal of being self-sustaining is essential to human space exploration. Valuable inputs are coming directly from space research that are applicable to Earth, which means space exploration helps the Earth.

Barbara Imhof   The goal, then, should be to build cities like spaceships, completely self-sustaining. And when we have mastered this, we will be able to build technological biospheres anywhere in the universe. We can build spaceships as cities.

Deep Space

In space we recognise our limits. We put ourselves in a situation where those limits are hard. We only have so much water, so much mass, so much volume and we need to work within these constraints. That mindset is essential for designing for Earth as well.

Christina Ciardullo, Founder + Principal Architect SEArch+,
Researcher Yale Center for Ecosystems + Architecture
(Radio Orange Space Specials: Reciprocities: the Earth–space continuum, 13 May 2021)

Mars

Moon

Orbit

Earth Land
Earth Ocean

I very much believe that architects need to design the whole process. They can't just be concerned about designing a fixed, finished product because the product, as we all know, is never finished… we have to design the whole process, how the building is going to go up, how it's going to come down. We have to design the construction of it and the deconstruction of it. And, that's all part of the design.

A. Scott Howe, Senior Systems Engineer and Space Architect,
NASA's Jet Propulsion Laboratory
(Radio Orange Space Specials: MOBITAT – Transformers, 13 Nov 2007)

Designing for Outer Space:
An Extreme Environment

The thickness of the welded aluminium pressure shell of the International Space Station (ISS) measures only 4.8 mm. Standing off from the pressure shell, additional, thin material layers complete the protective shield against micrometeoroids and orbital debris while providing thermal insulation for the humans and machines that populate its interior. These surprisingly thin layers that make up the habitable modules' hull constitute the protection barriers between astronauts and the vacuum environment of low Earth orbit.→ p. 113

Outer space is considered to be the most extreme environment so far identified as a place that humans could inhabit. Designing for such extreme environments teaches us how to deal with the complex scarcity issues in a resource-constrained world.[1] With its successful history of providing a habitat for numerous astronauts and cosmonauts in outer space the ISS represents an archetype of space design, of which certain elements will continue to be referenced in future habitat designs. In redesigning the favourable conditions of Earth in outer space, Space Architecture studies and designs living and working environments for the survival of humans in the extreme.[2] These environments can and will support crews, bases, settlements, towns and cities in orbital microgravity → p. 113 and in partial gravity on the Moon,→ p. 85 Mars → p. 47 and beyond. In order to protect human life, decades of research has tested living at the extreme for extended periods of time.

Working Method and Approach

All architectures planned for orbit and other planetary surfaces are dependent on extensive, multidisciplinary collaboration between engineers, astronauts, scientists and architects.[3] A human space exploration project is an international, intercultural and interdisciplinary effort generating working methods that require sensitivity and multifaceted curiosity extending beyond architecture. To imagine, conceive, design and contribute to building human-tended bases in orbit or on planetary surfaces is, even within the most stringent constraints, an exciting remit for architects. The LIQUIFER team of Space Architects and systems engineering consultants reconfigures according to the requirements of each contracted project, working mainly within multidisciplinary European research projects or as a subcontractor for European Space Agency (ESA) contracts.

Engineers often perceive architectural design to be aesthetically driven, rather than recognising it as closer to systems engineering in practice.[4] In outer space, engineering requirements frequently prevail over architectural design. The work of Space Architects is a constant negotiation between human-centred design and the structural, mechanical and material requirements of extreme environments, with the aim of enabling safe and comfortable habitability in extreme thermal and pressure conditions, while fulfilling transportation requirements.[5]

In the extreme space environment, humans are continuously dependent on a suitably protective habitat. LIQUIFER works on the development of habitation modules and bases, and their related construction methods, mission designs and human factors. Designing for outer space encompasses interrelationships between technology, engineering, space and humans. Therefore, architects must incorporate all possible relationships into their designs: human–human, human–space, human–machine and machine–space.[6] These complex interactions are significant design drivers for human performance and comfort. Mission success is dependent on the integration of humans and technologies on board or in base. Space Architects facilitate this success when they design beyond the mere point of survival towards an environment where astronauts can thrive.

Environmental Influences on Design

In outer space we are faced with a number of environmental factors that significantly differ from habitable locations on Earth, these include: partial or microgravity → p. 131 (depending on planetary size or orbital speed), temperature extremes (dependent on distance and exposure to the Sun), pressure differences (dependent on presence and thickness of an atmosphere), micrometeoroid hazard (when atmosphere is thin or lacking) and exposure to high levels of radiation (without the protection of a magnetic shield). These distinct environmental conditions affect design and material choices and demand a new perspective from architects.

The impact of all of these environmental conditions have led to engineering and architectural standards that accommodate human physiology and psychology as best as possible. Interiors in which humans can survive are the result of a meticulous plan of all aspects of the environment. Onboard life support systems → p. 135 regulate temperature and pressure to create a familiar Earth-like atmosphere. Additionally, design solutions are impacted by factors we are usually protected from on Earth such as a requirement to guard against micrometeoroid strikes. The design of architecture for microgravity → p. 131 radically differs from the design of architecture for Earth or other planetary surfaces. No surface is differentiated—resulting in no true ceiling, floor or walls—but each can be equally accessed and occupied. The rules of terrestrial architecture no longer apply, meaning architects must consider interior space from a new bodily perspective.

Design Strategies for Resource Efficiency

In the extreme environments of outer space, resources and habitable space are restricted as a direct result of the limited capacity of rockets. In the past transportation costs from Earth into low Earth orbit amounted to tens of thousands of US dollars per kilogram of payload. Although recent commercial launch infrastructure has substantially reduced costs, resupply and material choices still run with an "every kilo counts" mentality. In addition, dynamic launch loads must be considered within the design of any component sent to space, which requires lightweight but very robust material and construction solutions. Material choices for human spaceflight must comply with a range of safety requirements, where toxicity, flammability and outgassing (the release of gases by a material) are of major concern.[7]

So far orbital architecture has acted as a testbed but, with each varied extreme environment encountered in outer space, a new set of parameters need to be taken into account that affect transport, construction and habitability. Spacecraft and space station design have different spatial parameters in comparison to stationary architectures planned for the surface of the Moon or Mars. Orbital architecture is generally modular and fully prefabricated, its size is largely determined by the size of the transport vehicle payload shroud, the part of the spacecraft that shield's the storage hold. In the International Habitation Module (I-Hab), the habit module of ESA's forthcom-

I-Hab → p. 118

ing Lunar Gateway space station, the total liveable space for four astronauts is restricted to less than 50 m³. Highly limited spaces result in design strategies that encompass multi-functional, transformable → p. 80 systems involving foldable furniture and room segments or deployable habitat envelope structures. → p. 52 In future, as larger rockets with greater volume and loading capacity become available, it is likely that transport, habitable space and resources will become less restrictive.

The vast distances that must be overcome to reach the planned destinations of long-duration spaceflight directly affect the feasibility of supplying and resupplying materials. Whilst the Moon, our closest neighbour, can be reached within a few days, a journey to Mars will take months. Therefore, the potential to use local resources during space missions has become an urgent area of research.

In-Situ Resource Utilisation, the use of locally available material and energy, sets the parameters for Lunar or Martian surface settlements. Regolith, the surface material of the Moon → p. 85 and Mars, → p. 47 is proposed as a multi-use material to be processed to create infrastructure such as roads for transportation as well as radiation shielding for habitable spaces. Local accessibility of water and energy is key for future long-term missions. Feasibility studies and prototype research is building on autonomous preparatory processes so that humans will find fully operable infrastructure when they arrive on Mars or the Moon.

Closing Loops: Questions of Sustainability

The same sustainable development objectives of creating safer, healthier and more circular economies in the built environment on Earth are shared with the development of closed-loop habitation systems for space.[8] Recycling is a mandatory factor when designing for extreme environments and outer space. When parts break or malfunction, they are considered for future use through upcycling or downcycling. A long-term goal when designing for space is to reuse spacecraft material as feedstock for additive manufacturing processes in order to produce new items in-situ on the Moon and Mars.

Onboard the ISS, oxygen and potable water are largely recovered. Advances in recovery systems which ensure 100 percent circularity has been the goal of many human spaceflight R&D projects. Greenhouses have been allocated an essential role in long-term human missions for local food production. The EDEN-ISS prototype explored plant growth in extreme environments within a shipping container-sized greenhouse that was stationed in Antarctica

EDEN-ISS → p. 146

for a number of years. Upscaling food culture systems is considered paramount for the successful establishment of bases on the Moon and Mars.

The Space Architect's Agenda

Human-inhabited modules in outer space are a primary example of design and architecture in extremely hostile environments. Buildings and the cosmos have always existed in relation to one another;[9] buildings *in* the cosmos will be relational to their very particular surroundings. Beyond scientists and engineers developing machines to stabilise basic environmental conditions for the survival of humans, the role of the Space Architect in the collaborative network is to deal with the basic ergonomic and psychological requirements of humans in these extreme conditions.

When LIQUIFER approaches a design project or feasibility study, we are striving to develop novel, supportive, resource-efficient approaches for long-duration spaceflight. Beyond making a habitable environment tolerable, we approach design with one eye on the development of an intelligent, comfortable environment that cares for its inhabitants, while protecting resources towards a closed-loop ecosystem.

LIQUIFER · Deep Space

Mars
44

Moon

Orbit

Earth Land
Earth Ocean

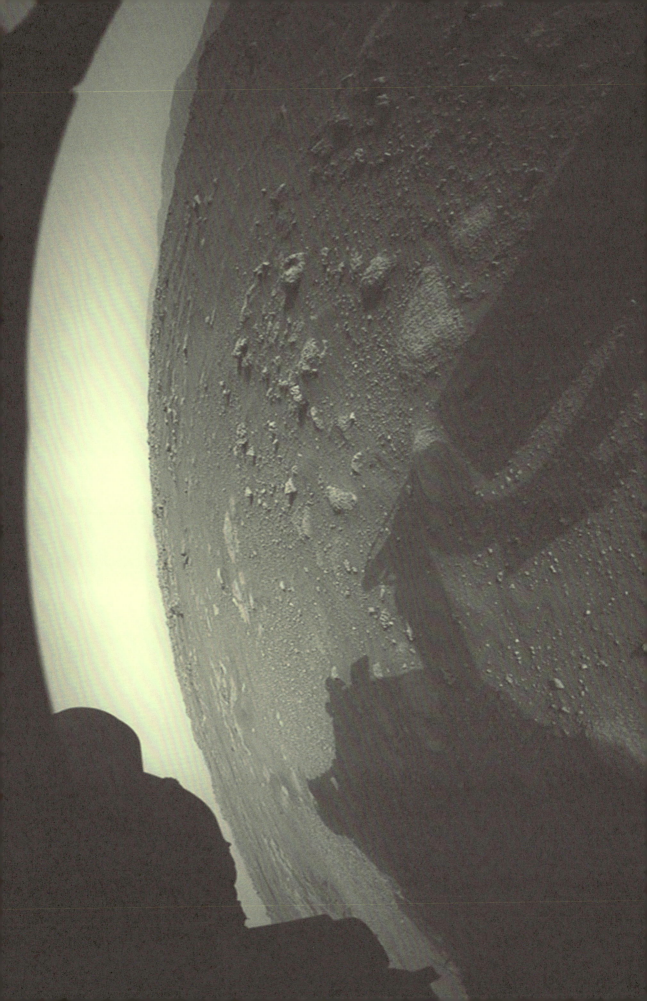

Mars

General characteristics

Mars is the fourth planet in the solar system characterised by a rocky crust and an iron-rich core like Mercury, Venus and Earth. The Red Planet derived its historic epithet from the large swathes of iron-rich dust driven over the planetary surface by extreme winds, producing the characteristic reddish hue we can see from Earth. The rocky formations, boulders and sediments that make up its surface have been shaped by historic volcanic activities, asteroid impacts, winds and the presumed presence of liquid surface water billions of years ago. Low gravity and lack of mobile plate tectonics resulted in the emergence of Olympus Mons, the tallest volcanic mountain in the solar system, standing at 21 km. At the same time, Martian topography is characterised by the largest canyon of the solar system, the Valles Marineris, a gigantic equatorial valley system, more than 4000 km long and up to 10 km deep.[1]

Atmosphere and magnetosphere

Mars is within the habitable zone, a zone defined by the distance from a star that allows the formation of liquid surface water under suitable atmospheric conditions.[2] 20 percent of the ancient Martian surface is thought to have been covered by ocean; at this time the atmosphere was believed to be thicker and the Martian climate warmer and wetter than it is today. It is likely that the interior of the planet progressively cooled to a point when the global magnetic field vanished, an effect that is associated with its small size.[3] Without a global magnetic field, Mars lost its shield against solar winds and over time, most of its atmosphere was stripped away by solar particle bombardment. The thinning of the atmosphere led to Mars' current state as a frozen planet, hostile to life. The orbit of Mars around the Sun is more elliptical than that of Earth, which leads to notably higher temperatures in the southern hemisphere during summer.[4] Resulting thermal imbalances are thought to cause extreme weather events like the giant dust storms that frequently engulf huge regions or even the entire planet.[5]

Space exploration

The utilisation of local resources → p. 106 is considered essential for long-term human presence on Mars. Water is accessible at the polar ice caps and by extraction from hydrated minerals.[6] In addition, there is increasing evidence that large amounts of ancient water may exist below the surface of the planet, specifically at the bottom of Valles Marineris.[7]

Solar energy is not expected to be the main source of energy on Mars due to its distance from the Sun as well as the hazard of large-scale, week-long dust storms. Currently, alternative energy sources are being researched. As carbon dioxide makes up almost 95 percent of the Martian atmosphere, biofuel could be produced with microbes that can consume, convert and upgrade carbon dioxide and water. This "biotechnology-enabled in-situ resource utilisation strategy" could produce 2,3-butanediol, a rocket propellant.[8]

Martian regolith contains vital nutrients for raising crops in Martian soil but high levels of toxic perchlorate compounds present in the soil could make produce unsafe for human consumption.[9] The composition of Martian regolith is considered viable for building purposes. Silicon dioxide, one of the most abundant compounds within this regolith,[10] will allow the production of glass-like building materials.[11]

	Mars	Earth
Mean Surface Gravity	3.71 m/s²	9.80 m/s²
Equatorial Diameter	6792 km	12756 km
Equatorial Circumference	21297 km	40030 km
Surface Pressure	6.36 mb	1014 mb
Length of Day	24.6 hours	24 hours
Length of Year	687 days	365 days
Temperature Extremes	−153°C to +20°C	−89°C to +57°C

Deep Space

LIQUIFER Projects for Mars

49—
77

Moon

Orbit

Earth Land
Earth Ocean

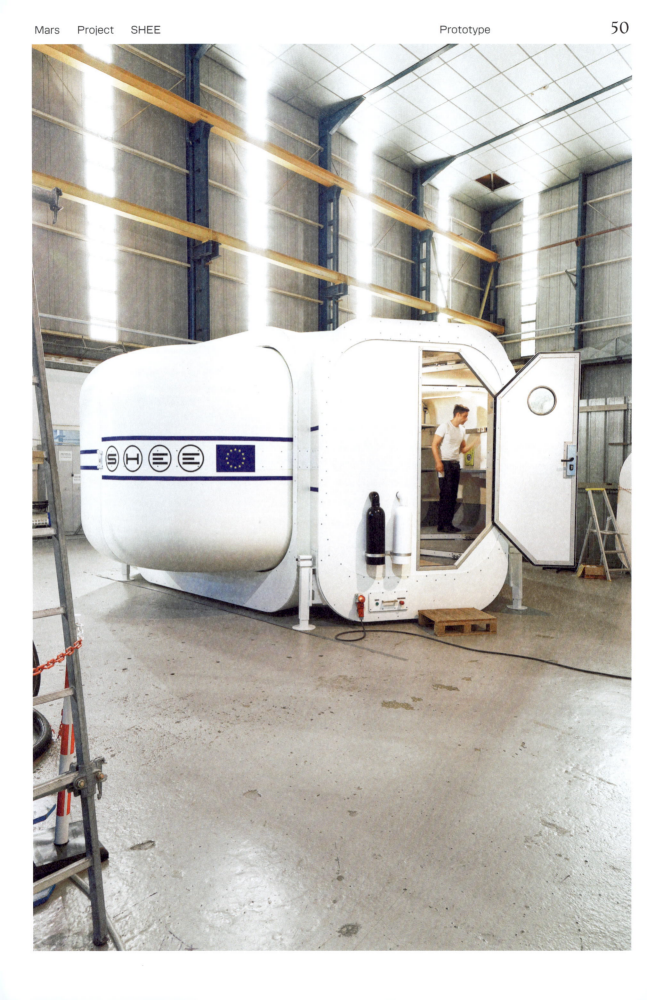

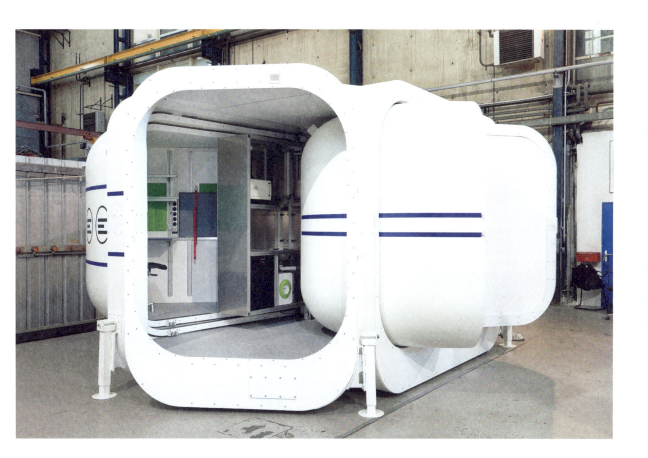

SHEE is an autonomously deployable habitat testbed
for human habitation in extreme environments.

SHEE (Self-deployable Habitat for Extreme Environments) is a habitable module designed for a planetary surface outpost. It was manufactured as a testbed for analogue simulations on Earth. The main objective of the project was to effectively integrate architecture and robotics in order to reduce volume during transportation and allow automated deployment of the fully outfitted unit before the astronauts' arrival. Two folded SHEE modules fit back-to-back into the cylindrical payload shroud of a rocket taking up only half the space of the fully deployed modules. Unique among analogue habitats, the SHEE design also fully complies with the requirements of standard transportation on Earth; in its folded configuration a single SHEE module does not exceed the dimensions of a high cube shipping container. The module was developed to be combined in a larger base configuration via docking ports and can be alternatively outfitted as habitats, laboratories, greenhouses, storage or medical units. The SHEE concept is also applicable in extreme terrestrial conditions as fully equipped medical or administrative emergency units for disaster mitigation.

The fabricated SHEE version was configured as a habitat for a crew of two and a mission duration of two weeks. Within an extremely confined space, the interior configuration consists of a central area and meeting space as well as four separate compartments within the deployable segments that facilitate retreat on long-duration missions.

LIQUIFER was in charge of the module design and transformability of the envelope as well as the concept, manufacturing and integration of interior furnishing. The transformable interior configurations enable the integration of the collapsible hull shells for transport and allow multifunctional usage during operation. As technical coordinator LIQUIFER was responsible for the integration of all systems.

T   2013 – 2015

P   European Union – Seventh Framework Programme for Research and Technological Development (EU-FP7), in the frame of space

C   Consortium partners – International Space University, France; LIQUIFER Systems Group, Austria; Space Applications Services, Belgium; Institute of Technology, University of Tartu, Estonia; COMEX, France; Sobriety, Czech Republic; Space Innovations, Czech Republic

L   The SHEE mock-up has been presented as part of exhibitions in Cologne, Strasbourg and Vienna and serves as a demonstration and test facility at the campus of the International Space University in Strasbourg.

Mars Project **SHEE** Prototype

1. Central meeting area with galley, foldable table and environmental control and monitoring system
2. Crew cabin
3. Office workspace
4. Wet lab and hygiene cabin
5. Hatch
6. EVA suitports
7. Workbench
8. Storage

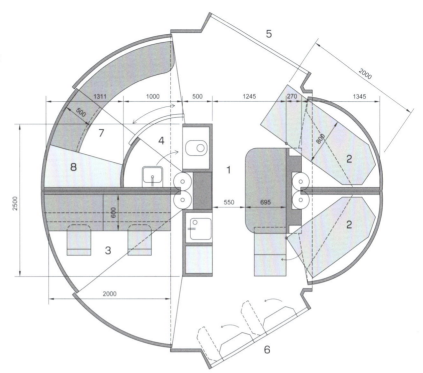

The SHEE module consists of a self-supporting central structure and four deployable compartments that are made from fibreglass foamcore shells with aluminium rims as reinforcement.

For transportation purposes the volume of the deployed configuration can be halved.

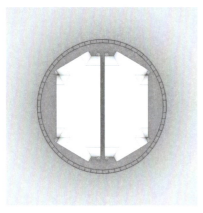
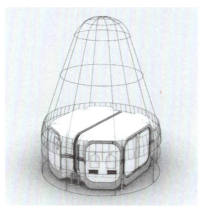

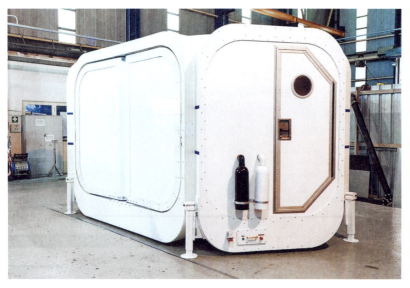

In its packed configuration two SHEE modules can be transported back-to-back in the payload shroud of a heavy lift launcher, and it complies with standard transport regulations on Earth.

Transformable interior furnishings can be compacted for the transport configuration and individually adapted when the module is in operation.

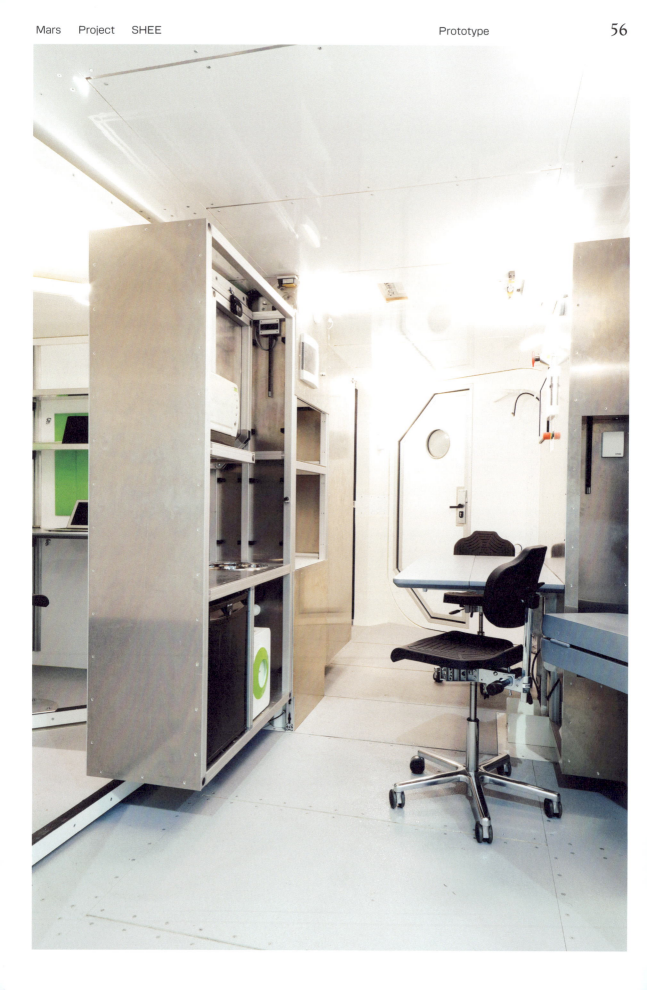

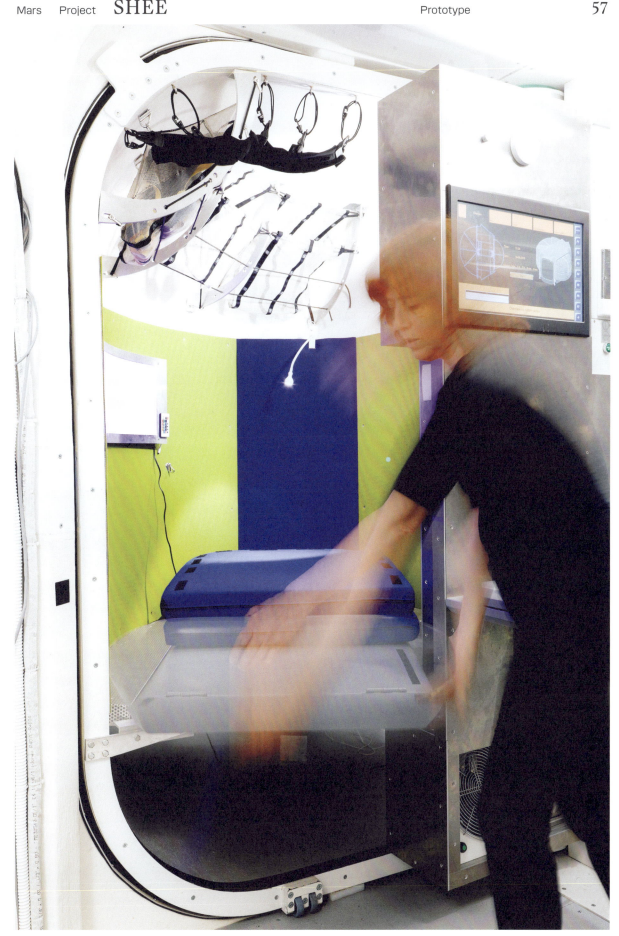

The centre of the habitat is the communal space where the crew prepares and eats their meals or conducts meetings, while easily monitoring the habitat subsystems.

A shelf system on both sides of the central space, retractable curtains and translucent folding walls provide visual screening for private activities in the deployable compartments.

In its folded configuration, the SHEE module can be transported to the simulation site on a flatbed truck. It is fully functional immediately after unloading and deployment.

SHEE was part of the Mars simulation campaign of the Moonwalk project at Rio Tinto in Spain where it served as local mission control centre with a suitport and laboratory.

Moonwalk developed scenarios and technologies for human-robot cooperation during planetary surface missions and tested the performance of the astronaut-robot team at two analogue sites on Earth. Simulation astronauts (simonauts) were supported by a small mobile assistant robot during Extravehicular Activities (EVA). The robotic rover was configured to autonomously follow the astronaut and support a variety of activities such as exploring terrain inaccessible to the astronaut or providing equipment for measuring and sampling activities. In addition the astronaut could actively direct the rover via control-by-gestures to perform desired activities. To simulate several exploration scenarios, → p. 175 the Moonwalk systems and technologies were tested at the acknowledged Mars → p. 126 analogue site at Rio Tinto, Spain. A second simulation → p. 188 was conducted underwater, → p. 183 offshore of Marseilles, to simulate Lunar gravity.

LIQUIFER designed a range of mission scenarios and developed corresponding mission procedures for astronaut-rover and astronaut-astronaut collaboration. To support selected mission scenarios, the team designed an exchangeable payload system for the rover chassis and several astronaut tools. The design included casings for measuring instruments, sample storage and tool fittings on the rover, as well as expandable and collapsible tools for the astronaut that reflect the restrictions of movement and visibility when wearing a heavy and bulky EVA suit during operation. In addition, LIQUIFER was responsible for the communication and dissemination of the project Moonwalk.

T 2013 – 2016

P European Union – Seventh Framework Programme for Research and Technological Development (EU-FP7), in the frame of space

C Consortium partners – DFKI Robotics Innovation Center, Germany; COMEX, France; EADS UK, UK; LIQUIFER Systems Group, Austria; Space Applications Services, Belgium; NTNU Centre for Interdisciplinary Research in Space, Norway; INTA Instituto Nacional de Técnica Aeroespacial, Spain

L Rio Tinto, Spain

Focussing on sampling and scouting activities, the Mars simulations in Rio Tinto compared astronaut-astronaut scenarios with astronaut-rover scenarios.

For each simulated mission scenario, SHEE provided the suitport interface for the simonaut's access to the heavy simulation spacesuit.

Mars   Project   Moonwalk   Prototype   67

The rover is either controlled by gestures or follows the astronaut. It carries an exchangeable payload box, sampling tools and a Raman spectrometer for the identification of bio-geological signatures.

Mars Project **Moonwalk** Prototype

With the help of the assistant rover, difficult terrain could be accessed and explored.

A set of manual sampling tools were designed to facilitate easy single-handed use by an astronaut. The Foldable Pick-up Claw and the Pantograph Sampling Tool were brought by the rover to the sampling site.

The head of the extendable Pantograph Sampling Tool combines the function of a shovel with a sealable sampling container. It can be released with a simple mechanism when repositioned on the payload box.

LavaHive is a modular Martian habitat design that applied the concept of "lava-casting", a 3D printing technology conceived by engineers from the European Space Agency (ESA) and the German Aerospace Center (DLR). In this concept, habitat hulls are made from regolith, the natural surface material on Mars, to protect against radiation and micro-meteorites. LavaHive is an example of in-situ resource utilisation →p.106 (ISRU), where materials and energy necessary for manufacturing and construction are sourced directly from the building site. In addition to the use of natural Martian resources, the project proposes the reuse of flight infrastructure for construction, so that after the entry vehicle has landed the back-shell would become part of recyclable onsite resources. LavaHive was conceived as a multifunctional facility consisting of a main habitation unit, airlock module, maintenance workshop, docking ports, laboratory and greenhouse.

LIQUIFER was responsible for the overall design of the Martian base. The team also developed the interior design, the visualisation of the project and provided a 3D printed architectural model.

LavaHive was the first ISRU-focused project undertaken by LIQUIFER. It influenced the project RegoLight →p.90 in developing scenarios and designs for solar-sintered shelters on the Moon.

T   2015
P   Third Prize in the NASA 3D-Printed Habitat Challenge Competition, 2015 World Maker Faire New York, USA
C   Consortium partners – European Space Agency & European Astronaut Centre, Germany; LIQUIFER Systems Group, Austria

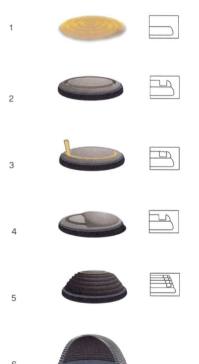

1   Molten regolith foundation
2   Sintered regolith channel
3   Channels filled with molten regolith
4   Next regolith layer
5   Repeat on upper layers
6   Remove loose regolith

Mars Project LavaHive — Concept Design

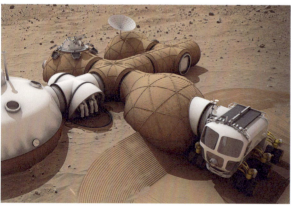

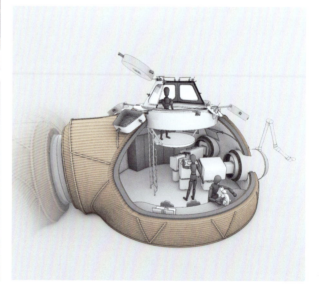

LavaHive is a multifunctional outpost proposal for the Martian surface. The concept builds on recycled spacecraft materials and 'lava-casting', a novel construction technique utilising in-situ regolith.

LavaHive

Concept Design

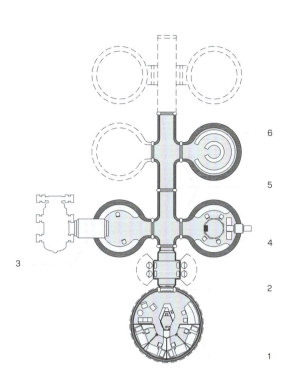

1. Habitat
2. Node: airlock and suitports
3. Maintenance workshop, docking ports and pressurised vehicles
4. Laboratory: cupola, sample experiments and glove box
5. Security hatch
6. Greenhouse

Possible LavaHive configurations.

Floor plan of the habitat with the communal dining and living area, four individual crew quarters and the hygiene station in the centre.

Mars · Project · FASTER · Prototype

FASTER (the Forward Acquisition of Soil and Terrain for Exploration Rover) was the development of an alternative method of collecting planetary surface information from an unknown terrain during robotic exploration missions. Due to the relative sparsity of data about the Martian surface, the risk of restricted or lost manoeuvrability is a major challenge for robotic surface exploration. The rover may be impeded by a stretch of soft sand or other unforeseen obstacles.

To allow the rover to travel at higher speeds, the consortium developed methods for efficient in-situ testing of soil and terrain properties. The FASTER system employs and advances the concept of two cooperating rovers. It combines the features of a small all-terrain scout rover which can quickly and efficiently test the trafficability of terrain and a lightweight sensor tool attached to the front of the large ExoMars mother rover.

LIQUIFER was responsible for the coordination of the system requirements and interfaces, in addition to the development of sensor tools that fit to the chassis of the mother rover. Two concepts were designed: the "Wheeled Bevameter" and the "Pathbeater". The Wheeled Bevameter concept was built as a mockup and tested at the premises of Airbus in Stevenage, UK. In addition LIQUIFER contributed to the project communication, and visualisation including a video documentary of the project. The robotic mission scenarios of FASTER provided valuable insights for the Moonwalk project's human-robot cooperation scenarios.

T   2011 – 2014
P   European Union – Seventh Framework Programme for Research and Technological Development (EU-FP7), in the frame of space
C   Consortium partners – DFKI Robotics Innovation Centre, Germany; University of Surrey, UK; Astrium, France; Space Applications Services, Belgium; LIQUIFER Systems Group, Austria; Astri Polska, Poland

Indoor FASTER Simulation Testbed trialled at the Airbus Mars Yard in Stevenage, UK.

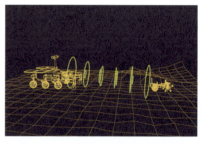
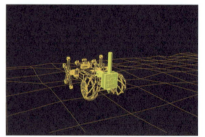
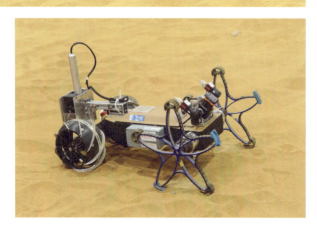

FASTER involves two cooperating robotic rovers. A small scout rover explores the soil and terrain properties to support the larger ESA ExoMars rover to traverse safely.

Mars Project **FASTER** Prototype

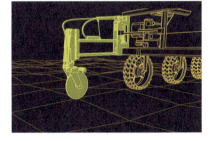

The mother rover is equipped with the Wheeled Bevameter, a soil sensor tool attached to the front of the rover. It analyses on-site bearing strength, shear strength and wheel slippage.

Deep Space

If we digitise the process of constructing or deconstructing a building, we need to consider the possibility of parts that move themselves into position. That simple piece not only takes care of its own geometry, but it takes care of its own movement as well, this is a very important aspect in the design.

A. Scott Howe, Senior Systems Engineer and Space Architect,
NASA's Jet Propulsion Laboratory
(Radio Orange Space Specials: MOBITAT – Transformers, 13 Nov 2007)

Mars

Moon

Orbit

Earth Land
Earth Ocean

We'll have to think about pieces that can be put together easily using robotic means, moving things x, y, z in space, rotating, and so forth. That is a part of our design process.

A. Scott Howe, Senior Systems Engineer and Space Architect,
NASA's Jet Propulsion Laboratory
(Radio Orange Space Specials: MOBITAT – Transformers, 13 Nov 2007)

The Pursuit of Adaptability

Transformability is the pursuit of adaptable design solutions, based on a 'less is more' approach. Its objectives are threefold: space-saving, multifunctionality, and the ability to create temporary spaces. LIQUIFER has implemented transformability into its designs as a means to multiply the potential of interior architectural elements, thus hacking the common limitations of available working and habitable space in elements such as habitats, vehicles and facilities.

Logics of transformability for design

There are a number of different, overlapping logics of transformation in design, which each demonstrate ways to save space. In all cases, transformable architecture addresses inherent limitations in both interior volume and missions' budgets.

Some solutions primarily aim to reduce the volume of an element while it is being transported, prior to its use. Architecture designed for space missions is either dependent on once-in-a-lifetime deployment or can be designed to allow it to be repeatedly deployed and collapsed, resulting in adaptable, responsive and flexible solutions. Architecture for outer space is often designed to have structural elements that autonomously deploy.

Other solutions aim to save space while in use or between uses. Changing the layout of an interior space without affecting the size of the volume is a common design choice in fixed volumes such as the International Space Station (ISS) or the planned Gateway I-Hab platform. The limitations of interior volumes in the extreme environment of space challenge the architect to optimise the habitable space in a way to allow for alternative uses through the design of adaptable and multifunctional interior spaces.

LIQUIFER has designed multifunctional environments as a response to logistical constraints, such as the need to reuse spaces for diverse activities, and to provide psychological benefits, including maximising astronauts' privacy.

Designing transformability for transportation

The SHEE → p. 52 habitat was designed as a deployable structure to increase the amount of modules that could be transported within a rocket payload shroud. The habitat doubles in volume from its stored configuration to full deployment, with full interior outfitting contained within at all times. The design concept of the SHEE is based on a sequential deployment of rigid shell segments that are stabilised by pressurised sealing. For the purposes of on-Earth transportation, and repeated deployment and relocation, the habitat complies with the dimensions of a high-cube shipping container. When compacted for transportation, interior furniture is partly folded to accommodate the collapsible shell segments within the core structure. Collapsible furnishings also enable multifunctional usage of the interior space during operation. All sensitive, complex systems such as the life support systems → p. 135 are fixed and pre-installed in the non-deployable core.

Designing transformability for multiple uses of space

Dual- or triple-use areas can enhance the use and differentiation of space for astronauts. The habitat design for the RAMA → p. 98 mobile research laboratory was defined by the need for a pressurised rover which serves astronauts as a mobile habitat, refuge, workshop and research laboratory for advanced mission applications on the Moon → p. 85 and Mars → p. 47. The design concept incorporates multiple interior configurations that allow astronauts to perform daily tasks and work in the highly confined interior space of a vehicle. Seats attached to robotic arms are designed for smooth transformations from driver seat to work stool to meeting chair to lounge chair. The central meeting table can merge with the ground floor to cover access to the sleeping area and storm shelter below.

Designing transformability for privacy

Privacy is not just a personal, individual need but also a need that is shared among teams and groups.[1] Private areas in space stations are limited and primarily designed for the purpose of sleeping. Often crew quarters additionally function as a retreat from shared social spaces. Deployable crew quarters in the Gateway I-Hab → p. 118 were designed to retract with a telescopic mechanism during the day enabling the space to be used for other activities. The Deployable Getaway → p. 124 is an example of a collapsible, soft architecture that provides temporary crew quarters for astronauts during crew exchange periods at the ISS.

LIQUIFER   Deep Space

                                                                                               Mars

                                                                                               Moon
                                                                                                        82

                                                                                               Orbit

                                                                                               Earth Land
                                                                                               Earth Ocean

The Moon

General characteristics

The Moon is the sole natural satellite of planet Earth. According to the Giant Impact theory, the Moon formed when Earth collided with a Mars-sized celestial body.[1] When it formed, the Moon was much closer to Earth and currently spirals away by a few centimetres every year.[2] The Moon's rotation is synchronised so that the same side of the Moon is always facing Earth. Surface gravitation → p. 131 on the Moon is equal to one-sixth of the gravitation on Earth. Due to its substantial size in relation to Earth, the Moon moderates the Earth's wobble on its axis.[3] Its gravitational pull stabilises the Earth's climate and causes the ocean's tidal movements.

The surface of the Moon is characterised by impact craters, some of them hundreds of kilometres in diameter, generated by collisions with asteroids, comets and meteoroids. The solid rocky crust is covered by regolith, a shattered material which includes fragments of local bedrock, meteoroid debris and solar particles. Micrometeoroid impacts continue to erode the Lunar landscape. More than 3 billion years ago the dark zones of the Moon we see from Earth formed: the colour stems from rising magma, a dark iron-rich basaltic material. The lighter-coloured highlands are older and characterised by a heavily cratered terrain of anorthositic rock.

Atmosphere and magnetosphere

The atmosphere of the Moon is negligible, commonly referred to as an exosphere or a vacuum. The Moon's lack of atmosphere and magnetosphere leaves the Lunar surface unprotected against micrometeoroid bombardment, solar particle events and cosmic radiation. Lunar regolith is sharp-edged and electrically charged, and therefore highly abrasive and clings to other materials. Lunar dust is lifted from the surface by electrostatic levitation creating the 'horizontal glow' that was described by the Apollo astronauts.[4] Without the moderating effects of an atmosphere, temperature differences are extreme.

Space Exploration

Returning to the Moon is a primary goal in the re-establishment of long-duration human presence in space. The Lunar South pole is considered a feasible location for the first crewed outpost, as it has continuous access to solar energy and permanently shadowed regions with water ice deposits. Other regions away from the poles need to cope with the extensive period of darkness of a Lunar night, which lasts equivalent to 14 days on Earth. Water is also expected to be harvested from Lunar regolith via additional energy sources. Such sources are required for large-scale resource harvesting and mining operations. Apart from the planned application of nuclear fission technology,[5] the harvesting of Helium-3, deposited by Solar winds, is envisioned as a clean source of energy for nuclear fusion technology.[6]

Lunar regolith is considered the main in-situ building material → p. 106 for the construction of large shelters for protection against solar winds, cosmic radiation and micrometeoroids. Experiments in 2022 demonstrated that, despite stressful conditions for growing plants, it is possible to grow food crops in Lunar regolith.[7]

	Moon	Earth
Mean Surface Gravity	1.62 m/s²	9.80 m/s²
Equatorial Diameter	3474.8 km	12756 km
Equatorial Circumference	10917 km	40030 km
Surface Pressure	3×10^{-15} bar	1.014 bar
Length of Day	655.7 hours	24 hours
Temperature Extremes	−250°C to +127°C	−89°C to +57°C

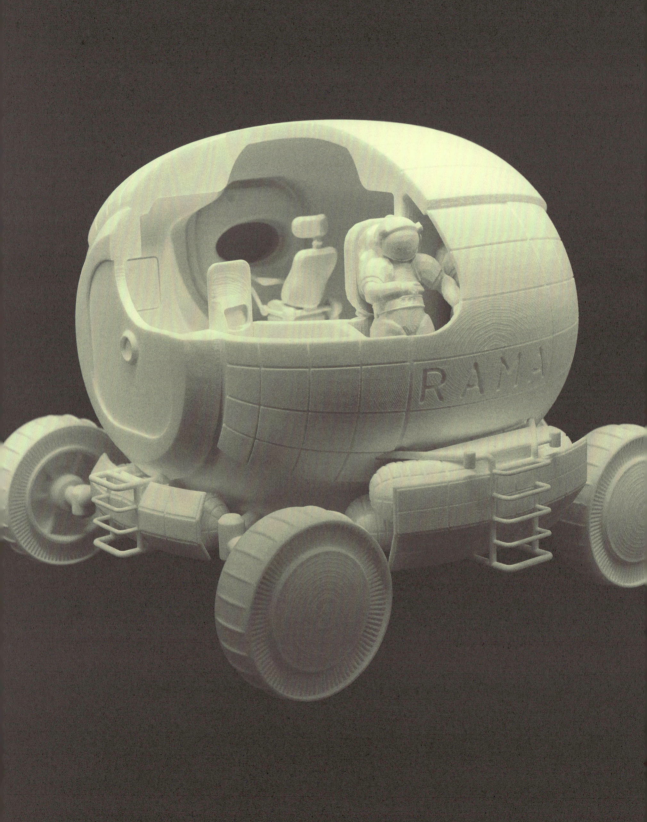

Deep Space

Mars

LIQUIFER Projects for the Moon

87—103

Orbit

Earth Land
Earth Ocean

RAMA is a mobile research laboratory for future
human space missions on the Moon.

RegoLight investigated utilising two abundantly available resources on the Moon, regolith and sunlight, for the automated fabrication of solid building elements. Regolith is the shattered material that naturally covers the Lunar surface and unobstructed sunlight is accessible during Lunar daytime, due to the absence of a Lunar atmosphere. RegoLight enhanced the additive layer manufacturing (ALM) technique of solar sintering Lunar regolith for in-situ building purposes → p. 106 and advanced the Technology Readiness Level (TRL) from a TRL3 to TRL5. For testing purposes, a Lunar soil simulant was used which mimicked the characteristics of Lunar regolith. Sintering of Lunar regolith simulant was demonstrated in alternative set-ups using a movable printing table or a mobile printing head. In addition, solar sintering was demonstrated inside a vacuum chamber. The project produced finite element models and conducted mechanical property tests which fuelled architectural scenarios.

LIQUIFER was responsible for scenario development and contributed exemplary designs for a Lunar base. The scenarios and designs primarily address infrastructure elements for micrometeoroid shielding, radiation shielding and dust mitigation which included habitats, levelled terrains and launchpads. LIQUIFER explored the potential of 3D printing to fabricate interlocking building elements that would enable construction without requiring binding material to be supplied from Earth. As part of an iterative design process, LIQUIFER investigated multiple building element geometries for a wide range of applications. In addition, the team organised all outreach and dissemination activities.

T 2015 – 2018

P European Union – Horizon 2020 (EU-H2020) project, topic of 3D printing / advancement of TRL

C Consortium partners – German Aerospace Centre (DLR), Germany; Space Applications Services, Belgium; LIQUIFER Systems Group, Austria; COMEX, France; Bollinger Grohmann Schneider, Austria

Moon Project # RegoLight

Technology Development

Solar 3D printer with a mobile, lightweight Fresnel lens. Sunlight is concentrated through the moveable lens to heat Lunar regolith simulant on the table below.

Preliminary test results for solar sintering of Lunar regolith simulant with the use of the Mobile Printing Head System.

Solar sintering does not require any additional binder but creates solid parts by heating granular material to the point at which its particles bond.

Sintered samples in test geometries

Moon Project RegoLight — Technology Development

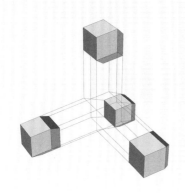

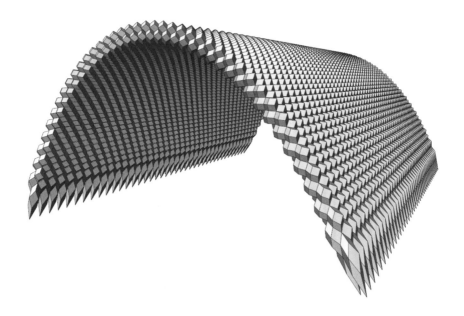

The concept of interlocking building elements has been extensively researched to avoid the use of any mortar during construction. After the form finding process, the rhombic dodecahedron was chosen as the basic geometry element.

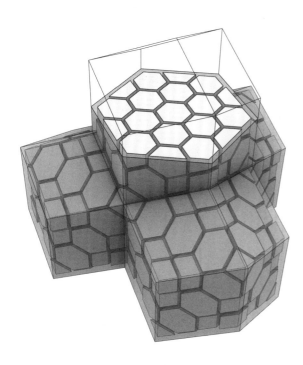

The infill of the building elements is a cell structure of printed chambers enclosing loose material.

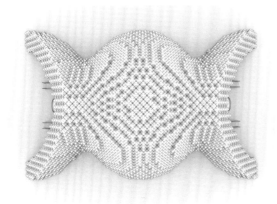
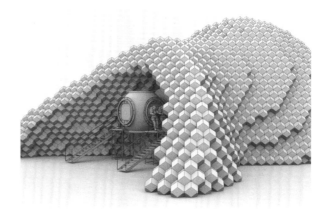

We started using the rhombic dodecahedron as a simple voxel to form various vault structures.

RegoLight

Technology Development

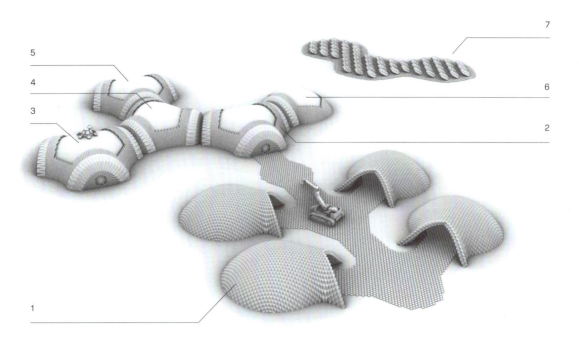

1 Hangars
2 Maintenance
3 Laboratory
4 Habitat
5 Greenhouse
6 Powerplant
7 Solar Array

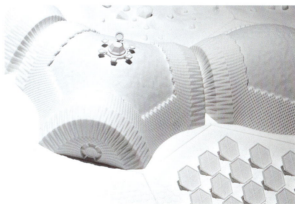

The Lunar south pole with its continuous access to solar light is envisaged as a promising site for a Lunar base.

Solar sintered building blocks are assembled to create self-supporting structures that provide shelter against deadly solar radiation and micrometeoroids.

Moon Project RegoLight Technology Development 96

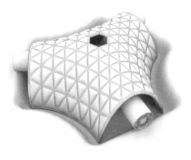
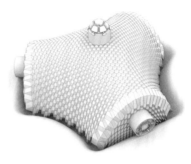

Dome Chamber
Pressurized Module Configuration

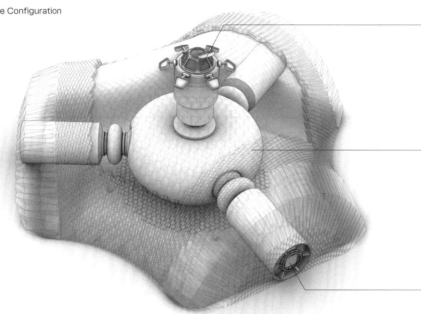

Cupola
optional 4 m Diameter

Inflatable
Toriod 2 Levels
approx. 650 m³

Transition Module
Rigid Cylinder
approx. 90 m³ each

The facility is composed of dome like protection shelters covering different types of pressurised modules. Each dome is made of 2-3 metre-thick walls composed of individually shaped building blocks.

RAMA (Rover for Advanced Mission Applications), a mobile research laboratory for the Moon and Mars, was designed in line with the scientific and operational requirements defined in the European Space Agency (ESA) Surface Architecture Study. The pressurised vehicle is configured to serve two astronauts as a habitat, refuge and laboratory during a 30-day journey on the Lunar or Martian surface. Fundamental issues such as habitability, human-machine interface, safety, dust mitigation, interplanetary contamination and radiation protection are factored into the design of RAMA. The acronym RAMA does not only define the purpose of the vehicle but is also a reference to Sir Arthur C. Clark's science-fiction work *Rendezvous with Rama*.

LIQUIFER was responsible for the concept design including engineering, a technology roadmap and the laboratory's associated costs. The vehicle size was defined by anticipated restrictions of the payload shroud. Transformable elements →p.80 are key features in the RAMA design: wheels fold below the vehicle cabin during transportation in the rocket. In the interior all required functions, such as the cockpit, laboratory workspace, galley, hygiene cabin, storage and suitports, are integrated along a central void that is continuously transformed by the alternating positions of two robotic chairs. The ergonomically adaptable chairs enable multifunctional use and can be individually reconfigured to personalise the highly confined interior space. The integrated life support system (LSS) →p.135 is positioned below the floor around the central sleeping compartment, which also serves as a storm shelter that protects against elevated radiation levels. A layer of the circular door of the storm shelter can be lifted and transformed into a dining or meeting table.

T   2007 – 2009
P   European Space Agency project, under subcontract to Thales Alenia Space, as part of Surface Architecture Studies

Moon Project RAMA — Concept Design — 100

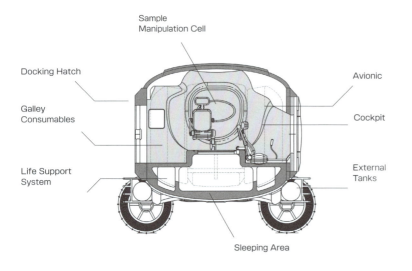
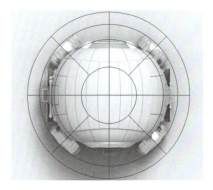

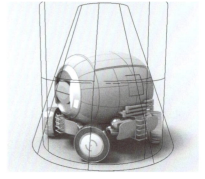

The interior configuration of the mobile research laboratory RAMA can be continually adapted with alternating positions of two robotic chairs.

The wheels of the rover can be folded in order to comply with the spatial limitation of the payload shroud in the rocket.

Smartie (Smart Resource Management based on Internet of Things to support off-Earth manufacturing of Lunar infrastructures), an ESA-funded feasibility study led by LIQUIFER, investigated how to assure self-sustainable long-duration missions on the Moon. This off-Earth manufacturing architecture is based on a combination of additive manufacturing (AM) technologies and the creation of an autonomous Internet of Manufacturing Things (IoMT).

Operational bottlenecks can be identified in autonomous IoMT technology, allowing in-situ resource utilisation →p. 106 and recycling processes to be optimised to efficiently maintain Lunar infrastructure. Additive manufacturing infrastructure on the Lunar surface would be connected to a data cloud as part of a wider Lunar satellite network, like those envisioned in ESA's Moonlight and NASA's LunaNet. In the initial phase, a mirror cloud would be established on Earth to resupply the Lunar base. The long-term goal is to establish a large, autonomous and sustainable Lunar base.

LIQUIFER led the feasibility study and was responsible for establishing the user requirements and Smartie architecture. LIQUIFER supported use cases for smart data management that incorporated AM technology and recycling processes. The project was communicated with an animation and visuals.

T   2021

P   European Space Agency project, under the ESA Open Space Innovation Platform

C   Consortium partners – LIQUIFER Systems Group, Austria; OHB System AG, Germany; Spartan Space c/o BC ESPACE ENTREPRISES, France; Azimut Space GmbH, Germany; Zühlke Engineering GmBH, Austria

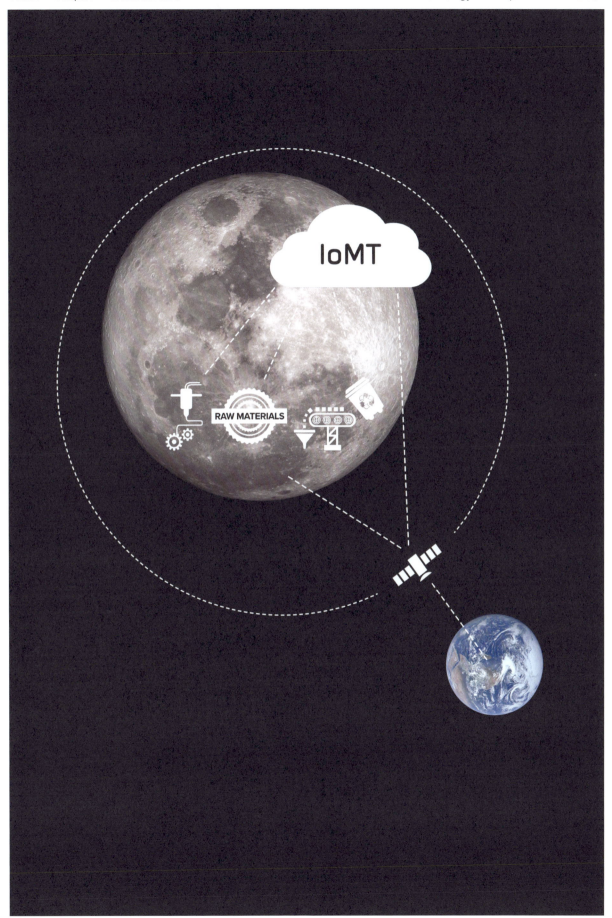

Deep Space

One of the most important aspects of growing our capability in operations and settlement in these remote places is how we can build what we need from what we find where we go.

Brent Sherwood, Senior Vice President for Advanced Development Programs, Blue Origin
(Radio Orange Space Specials:
Could we prevent people from going to the Moon or Mars? 15 Aug 2006)

Mars

Moon

Orbit

Earth Land
Earth Ocean

The extraction of resources is going to be a lot about sifting out rare grains in the regolith that contain valuable minerals. We have to get really good at excavating the regolith, transporting it, processing it and sorting it to enrich those rare components that are valuable. The technologies from mineral processing in terrestrial mining are going to be extremely important to extract valuable resources from the Moon, Mars and asteroids.

Kevin Cannon, Planetary Geologist, Colorado School of Mines
(Radio Orange Space Specials: Habitats on Moon and Mars
built from local material, 14 May 2022)

The New Vernacular in Outer Space

A new vernacular architecture emerges from In-Situ Resource Utilisation (ISRU), the approach of utilising local resources and developing innovative technologies for the creation of habitable places in the extremes of outer space. ISRU is a fundamental strategy for long-duration spaceflight, which uses locally available materials for the construction and operation of infrastructure on planetary surfaces. The use of local materials in architecture is not a new strategy but one recurrent in traditions of vernacular architecture where materials and resources from the location impact the form, implementation of technologies and outcome of the built environment. These local architectures, inherently related to their landscapes, are built to meet specific needs whilst factoring in the local economy.

Economically, dependency on the resupply of materials and machines from Earth is not viable due to extortionate costs when launching rockets from Earth into low Earth orbit or beyond. Although commercial launch infrastructure has reduced costs substantially in recent years, launch costs remain a major limiting factor for the expansion of space exploration and planned commercial activities.[1] Furthermore, it is simply not feasible to transport the immense mass of material required to build a Lunar settlement from Earth to the Moon. Reducing costs is built into the concept of ISRU as materials from the Lunar or Martian surfaces are extracted, processed, manufactured and used on site, thereby ensuring sustained operations on location.

As Lunar and Martian inhabitants will mainly live indoors, the primary way to meet their needs will be through the provision of shelter, the generation of energy, water, oxygen and food. To pilot this set-up, the Moon will be used as a test site for future settlements on Mars.[2] Although Mars is richer in resources, the Moon will be utilised to develop autonomous off-Earth manufacturing and construction technologies required for sustainable future settlements. These technologies must reliably function by the time humans go to Mars, where continuous resupply is not feasible and autonomy will be considered a prerequisite. ISRU is enabled by robotics, artificial intelligence, networked systems, and additive manufacturing technologies such as 3D printing.[3] These technologies could enable autonomous operations such as the excavation, transportation, sorting and processing of surface material for the construction of shelters and the extraction and processing of water ice deposits to generate clean liquid water for human consumption or to produce propellants for transportation. ISRU will be a multi-stage process, meaning a material, equipment and energy continuum will first be put in place that relies on elements from Earth in combination with locally available resources. By the time settlements are in place, the goal is to rely extensively on what is available on the Lunar doorstep.

The primary building and construction material for Lunar and Martian settlements is regolith: a sand-like, loose surface material resulting from billions of years of impacts on rocky planets.[4] Although its composition varies throughout our Solar System, its abundance, as well as its shielding properties make it the material of choice for the future construction of massive shelters which can protect against harmful radiation and micrometeoroids.

RegoLight → p. 90

The development of the RegoLight solar sintering process aimed to increase technological readiness for off-Earth manufacturing purposes on the Moon. This process relies on solar energy, regolith and automated 3D printers to melt the surface of regolith particles in order to generate a solid building mass. RegoLight utilised this technology to form interlocking building elements, as sintered regolith exhibits significant resistance to compressive stresses.

Beyond the forms of building elements, mining and processing techniques of regolith, maintenance of machinery and in-situ energy generation are key for autonomous fabrication on the Moon. Following the technological advances of RegoLight, the Paving the Road project demonstrated how a large laser beam could be used to produce interlocking paving elements to create roads. Roads are the first step in the development of Lunar settlements as they will allow for easy trafficability and dust mitigation on the Lunar surface.

Beyond settlement construction technologies and in-situ materials, an autonomous Internet of Manufacturing Things (IoMT) that enables independence from Earth was proposed in Smartie. Once settlements are under

Smartie → p. 102

construction, the IoMT network would support a sustainable Lunar base through careful resource management and maintenance forecasting, applying ISRU principles to produce an efficient logistics plan. The network would repair and develop extra on-site infrastructure with a combination of resources from Earth and the Moon. As Lunar bases evolve, ISRU will recycle waste materials from the base to manufacture products needed for the development, maintenance and operation of the base.

By accommodating the values imposed by an ISRU approach, its defining principles can be applied to infrastructure on Earth, such as developing 3D printing technologies for low-cost housing and sourcing local materials for building and construction. The investment of time in scientific developments, technological advancements and closed-loop systems for low-waste-living in space environments will lead to applicable closed-loop systems for the built environment on Earth.

LIQUIFER

Given the environment on the Moon and Mars ISRU is a major challenge. When we look at Earth, we see we don't have much robotic construction, or ISRU construction here, even though a lot of the challenges that we see elsewhere on the other planetary bodies don't exist here. We have no worries about radiation, about oxygen, about resources, water, and yet our construction is still weighted towards manual labour with assistive technologies. That's sort of a sign that this is really, really hard to do, and it'll be an order of magnitude harder on a planetary body other than Earth.

*Haym Benaroya, Professor of Mechanical & Aerospace Engineering,
Rutgers University, (Radio Orange Space Specials:
Habitats on Moon and Mars built from local material, 14 May 2022)*

When creating a space in space, you need privacy where people can retreat. You need windows where they can look out at the heavens, a place where it is possible to see the Earth as a globe, as an entity, because that seems to be something that the astronauts really like doing.

*Nick Kanas, M.D., Professor Emeritus of Psychiatry
at the University of California, San Francisco
(Radio Orange Space Specials: Space Psychology and Psychiatry, 16 Jun 2009)*

LIQUIFER   Deep Space

                                                                      Mars

                                                                      Moon

                                                                      Orbit
                                                                      110

                                                                      Earth Land
                                                                      Earth Ocean

Orbit

General characteristics

Planets orbit around a sun and moon's orbit around planets. Orbits are possible if there is a balance between gravitational and centrifugal forces. Artificial satellites or space stations are placed in orbits with an adequate initial impulse to keep them orbiting. Thousands of artificial satellites orbit Earth in low Earth orbit (LEO)—a region approximately 160 km to 2000 km above sea level—with many more scheduled to be launched. Space stations, satellites and rockets launched from Earth comprise the active LEO infrastructure, which is increasingly threatened by potential collisions with space debris, including an accumulation of inactive satellites, remnants from rocket stages or natural meteoroid debris. Space exploration beyond LEO involves orbits around the Moon, Mars or other planetary bodies of the Solar System and beyond.

Atmosphere and magnetosphere

Objects in LEO are exposed to the very upper layers of the Earth's atmosphere which causes a slight atmospheric drag. The ambient pressure is extremely low. The International Space Station (ISS) orbits Earth every 90 minutes, at a distance of approximately 400 km and an orbital speed of 7.66 km/sec. At 400 km above sea level, the gravitation of Earth is compensated by the centrifugal forces at the orbital speed of the space station, resulting in a state of microgravity.

The ISS orbits at an altitude where astronauts are still shielded from harmful radiation due to the presence of Earth's global magnetic field. The high-speed subatomic particles emitted by the Sun are largely trapped in Earth's magnetosphere and held within the two Van Allen Belts. Space Stations orbiting around the Moon, as planned with Gateway, → p. 106 a multi-purpose outpost and staging point for future deep space exploration, are challenged with providing sufficient radiation protection for astronauts.

Temperatures in outer space could theoretically reach absolute zero between celestial bodies (0° Kelvin or −273°C). In addition to dramatic temperature ranges in a vacuum, no sound can be transmitted. All objects in this space are exposed to acute dehydration, a consideration affecting the survival of any lifeform within seconds.

Space Exploration

The sun is the main energy resource in LEO and provides sufficient power to operate the ISS. In deep space, solar energy needs to be supplemented by additional energy sources. Increasingly, it is envisioned that mineral-rich asteroids will be harvested to provide rare materials such as nickel, iridium, palladium, platinum, titanium and gold. In the long term, the European Space Agency aims to recycle space debris in LEO for orbital space manufacturing.[1]

	Gateway (Moon orbit)	ISS (Earth orbit)
Gravity (m/s²)	microgravity	microgravity
Orbit Period	7 days	90 mins
Altitude Range	1500–70 000 km	280–460 km
Mission Periods	30–90 days	c. 180 days
Interior Temperature Range	4–27 °C	18–23 °C
Exterior Temperature Extremes	−130°C to +120°C	−160°C to +120°C
Internal Pressurised Volume	125 m³	1000 m³

Deep Space

Mars

Moon

LIQUIFER Projects for Orbit   115—
127
Earth Land
Earth Ocean

Visualisation of the future Gateway orbiting the Moon.

I-Hab is part of the Gateway Lunar Orbital Platform, a space station dedicated to supporting missions beyond low Earth orbit, including future missions to the Moon and Mars. Gateway is a collaboration between the European Space Agency (ESA), NASA, Japan Aerospace Exploration Agency (JAXA) and the Canadian Space Agency (CSA), targeted for completion in 2028.

Stringent design parameters were derived from the launch capacities of rockets, spatial requirements for life support systems, → p.135 and the necessary support for a wide variety of activities for a crew of four during the proposed 30-day mission duration. Virtual architectural models allow designers to explore different spatial configurations and make iterative design developments in order to maximise the use of the module, which has an internal volume of 48 m³. A physical mockup was built at a 1:1 scale to provide a full-body immersive experience of the multi-purpose central volume, as well as the attached science workspace, galley and deployable crew quarters.

LIQUIFER was involved in the architectural design development and the configuration of the 1:1 mockup. Two teams were assigned in parallel by ESA to complete the design concept phase; one headed by Thales Alenia Space Italy (TAS-I) in Turin and the other led by Airbus Defence and Space in Bremen. LIQUIFER initially supported Airbus in architectural design development and in a later phase Thales Alenia Space Italy. The design presented here shows the early design phase for Airbus.

T   2018 – ongoing

P   European Space Agency under a subcontract to Airbus Bremen (2018-2019) and Thales Alenia Space (2020-ongoing)

C   Consortium partners – (2018-2019) Airbus, Bremen, Germany; Airbus, Friedrichshafen, Germany; Thales Alenia Space TAS-I, Italy; Sener, Spain; QinetiQ, Spain; Space Applications Services, Belgium; Airbus Crisa, Spain; LIQUIFER, Austria. (2020-ongoing) Thales Alenia Space TAS-I, Italy; LIQUIFER, Austria; Spartan Space, France

L   Near-Rectilinear Halo Orbit (NRHO) from 2028 onwards

Orbit Project # Gateway I-Habt Concept Design

Science Control

Galley

Stowage

Toilet

Crew Quaters

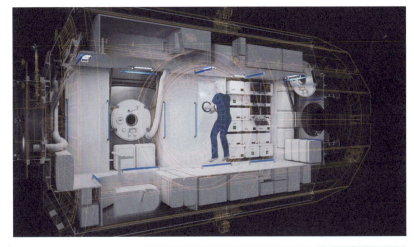

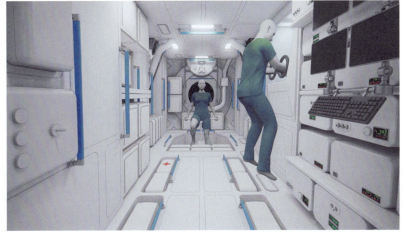

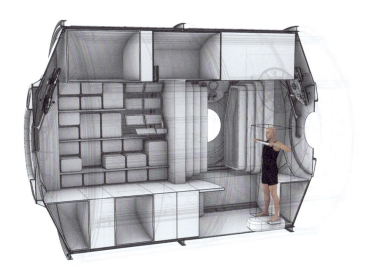

The layout represents the early I-Hab concept design
by LIQUIFER for Airbus. It was built as full-size
mock-up at the Airbus premises in Bremen, Germany.

Orbit   Project   Gateway I-Hab　　　　　　　　　　　　　　　Concept Design

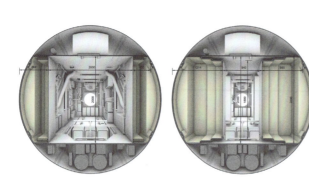

In microgravity all surfaces can accomodate functions, increasing the usability of a confined space. Deployable crew quarters in the I-Hab design provide additional space for alternative use.

1:1 Mock-Up of I-Hab for the first phase of the concept design study located at AIRBUS premises in Bremen, Germany.

Gateway I-Hab

Orbit Project — Concept Design — 121

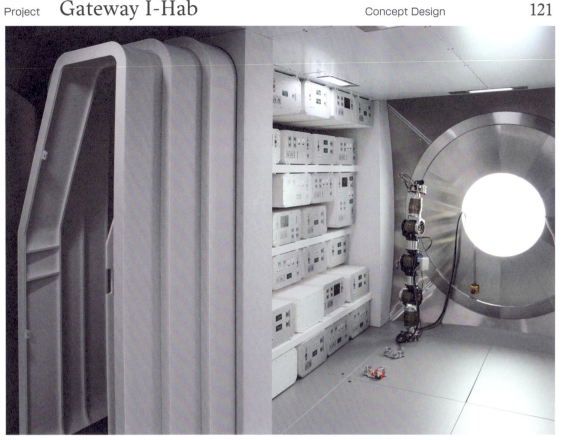

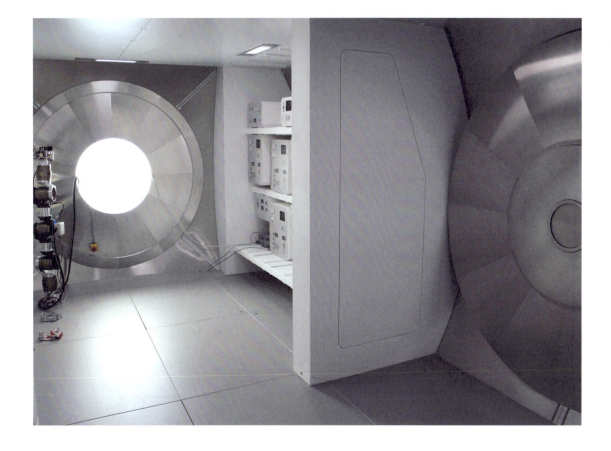

Orbit Project # Deployable Getaway Prototype 123

The Deployable Getaway provides a temporary private retreat for working, relaxing and sleeping on orbital space stations.

The Deployable Getaway is a collapsible crew quarter →p. 80 for use in microgravity →p. 131 orbital stations such as the International Space Station (ISS). It provides flexible setups for longer duration missions and intends to improve habitability for crew exchange periods. In contrast to the permanently integrated cabins, the Getaway can be positioned at any location on the space station to establish a private space suited to the individual preferences of the astronaut. It is conceived to provide a temporary retreat for relaxation, reflection and power naps that can lead to better health and safety for astronauts whose work demands consistent high performance.

A Deployable Getaway for office environments on Earth was developed simultaneously. Both designs have folding geometries in response to space limitations. But each requires substantially different ergonomic approaches for deployment, accessibility and body support. While the space Getaway is designed to be handled in microgravity, where it will be weightless, the terrestrial solution is designed to evenly distribute its weight. For the design of the space-based Deployable Getaway, the folding panels had to be sufficiently thick to meet the acoustic requirements for space stations. Space station hardware must isolate sounds to mitigate the risk of excessive noise travelling through the station but thicker, sound-dampening panels created challenges for the origami-like folds that allow the Getaway to collapse when not in use.

T 2007 – 2009
P LIQUIFER in-house project co-funded by the Austrian Aeronautics and Space Agency of the Austrian Research Promotion Agency as part of the 5th call of the Austrian Space Applications Programme

Folding sequence of the crewquarter cabin on the ISS.

Deployable Getaway

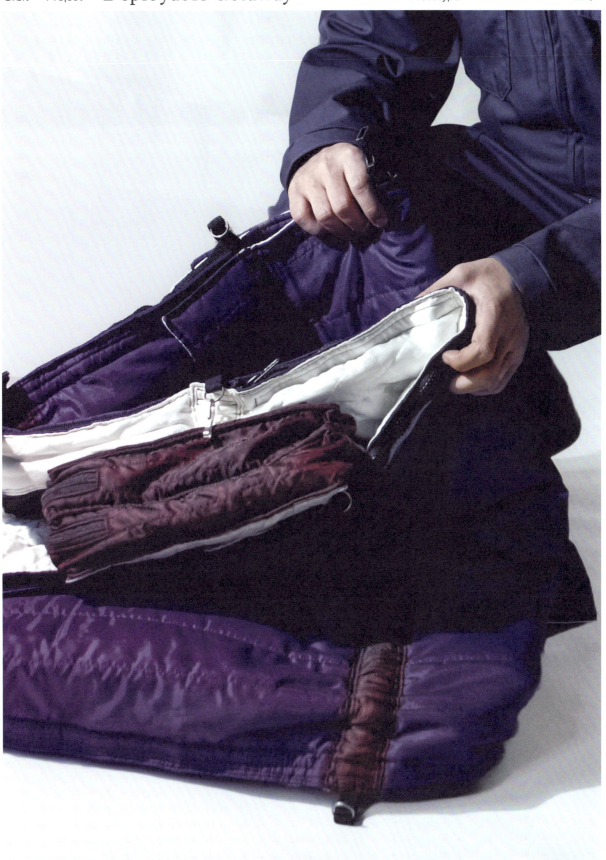

Orbit Project ISS – Sleep Kit Prototype 126

The ISS – Sleep Kit is a sleeping bag developed for microgravity and for use on the ISS. It is an advanced version of the design originally produced for the Deployable Getaway →p. 124 crew quarter. LIQUIFER conducted a design study with the goal of testing an alternative sleeping bag for microgravity, working closely with astronaut Gerhard Thiele. The ISS – Sleep Kit supports the neutral posture that a body tends to assume in microgravity while being attached to a structural element, an indispensable feature that prevents uncontrolled floating during sleep. In addition, individual temperature regulation is facilitated through a removable breast cover, as well as ventilation slots at the back and the feet. As back pain may occur due to a lack of weight on the spinal system, the sleeping bag includes access pockets to the lower back area for self-massage. LIQUIFER manufactured an ISS – Sleep Kit prototype with flight-certified Nomex-based textiles. It can be complemented with a lightweight silk lining and a hood to generate the familiar and calming sensation of using a cushion, which is otherwise not required in a microgravity environment. →p. 131

T 2010 – 2012
P LIQUIFER in-house project co-funded by the Austrian Aeronautics and Space Agency of the Austrian Research Promotion Agency as part of the 7th call of the Austrian Space Applications Programme
C Consultants: Gerhard Thiele, astronaut; Ulrich Kübler, Airbus Defence and Space
S Sponsors: IBENA; Velcro GmbH; 3M; Eduard Kupfer; Sanders GmbH & Co. KG; Michael Schultes experimonde

1 100% silk hood inlay attached to Nomex exterior with velcro.
2 100% silk sleeping bag inlay attached to Nomex exterior with velcro.
3 Velcro closure for inverted pleat.
4 Exterior sleeping bag made from Nomex. Expanded area at knees accommodates neutral body position.
5 Inverted pleat added to allow for more movement possibilities.

LIQUIFER   Deep Space

                                                              Mars

                                                              Moon

                                                              Orbit

                                                              Earth Land
                                                              Earth Ocean

In a gravity rich environment our natural state is a state of rest, and we have to actively move ourselves, we have to actively initiate movement to reach for a cup, to get out of a chair, to move across a room. In a microgravity environment our natural state is motion, as such we have to actively steady ourselves to create our static state; and, we have to actively secure objects in order to keep them in a resting position. So, we are completely flipping our relationship with our environment and objects in those two different situations.

Sue Fairburn, Design Researcher,
the Wilson School of Design/Principal, Fibre Design Inc.
(Radio Orange Space Specials: Designing from the Unfamiliar, 14 March 2015)

When the Natural State is Motion

When watching filmed records of astronauts floating in space, it quickly becomes clear that standard architectural parameters must drastically change when designing for microgravity environments. Because microgravity allows no reference to ground or ceiling, all surfaces and directions are equally accessible. The Space Architect responds to the potential of omnidirectional use by making every surface accommodating and useful at the same time. The design configurations accommodate mission-critical payload, life support systems, hygiene stations, sleeping quarters, and sufficient space for working, exercising, meeting and eating. Solutions respond to both lack of space and the extended possibilities enabled by microgravity.

The natural state for objects and humans in microgravity is motion; a cup will not stay on a table when placed there, nor will water stay in a cup. The securing and storing of things are key design drivers for microgravity spaces, as these things are otherwise moved by the slightest exterior forces. Materials, objects and humans are always in motion, unless secured. Securing solutions are achieved with the use of velcro, clips, duct tape, elastic bungees and magnets. Hygiene kits are velcroed to the wall, food and water are stored in pouches, and cutlery sticks to meal trays with magnets. In the case of loss, an on-Earth stowage team keeps a database of all objects onboard, including trash, and can direct astronauts to the location of an object.[1] Humans, like objects, must be attached to interior elements to remain in one place. In order to secure astronauts when sleeping, their sleeping bags are attached to the sides of their cabin or to any structure within a habitat module. When seated, astronauts stabilise themselves with restraints to achieve their desired position.

Movement through the interior of the International Space Station (ISS) relies on the use of the arms, not the legs, illustrating the physiological adaptations that occur in Orbit as the body adopts strategies other than those determined by gravity. Pulling themselves through laboratories, sleeping quarters, stowage modules or into the cupola, astronauts use handrails or stationary elements to propel themselves forward, to push themselves away or to become steady in space. Opposite to our usual resting state on Earth, microgravity is defined by motion. During a 30-minute tour of the ISS given by previous crew commander Sunita Williams, viewers are introduced to Node, the NASA sleeping quarters, where four of six sleeping cabins are arranged like compass points in the round of the node.[2] Viewers are invited into an individual sleep station, the most personalised area for each astronaut on the ISS. The soft interior (unlike the typically hardware lined modules) stores personal belongings such as notebooks, clothes, photographs and memorabilia in a number of pockets and velcro-secured bags, or attaches them to the "walls" of the booths with elastic.

Although astronauts have the pleasure of effortless movement through space with minor bodily impulses, some sensations cannot be felt in microgravity. Astronauts cannot experience the sensation of lying down. In microgravity, the naturally assumed posture during sleep feels like sitting and can be done in any direction, challenging the orientation of astronauts. Design decisions help to reorient astronauts in a place where up and down, left and right can quickly change with simple bodily movements, by setting a uniform direction for lighting, writing on the walls and computer monitors.[3] Design can create sensations that remind astronauts of life on Earth in order to enhance well-being. LIQUIFER designed the ISS Sleep Kit, → p. 126 a sleeping bag for microgravity, in response to reported experiences of interrupted sleep patterns by astronauts. The Sleep Kit reflects the neutral body posture assumed in microgravity and provides features for easy covering and uncovering. It also incorporates a silk-lined hood to imitate the sensation of a cushion. LIQUIFER applied a similar approach to a previous sleeping bag design as part of the Deployable Getaway, → p. 124 a collapsible crew quarter cabin for the ISS, which included alternative cushion designs. Design solutions for microgravity may mimic habits from Earth, to create "home comforts" through the memory of a sensation.

Exercise equipment for astronauts is important to mitigate the effects of microgravity such as loss of bone density and muscle mass. The bike, treadmill and weightlifting machine are installed in a way so no force is put onto the spaceship structure when astronauts are exercising. Each piece of the exercise equipment is adapted to microgravity. For instance, the bike does not require a seat and, instead, feet are clipped into pedals and a body harness is worn to secure the astronaut. Similarly the treadmill is redesigned with elastic straps which astronauts must wear over the shoulders and around the waist to keep their feet in contact with the running belt. Familiar designs are often adapted for the microgravity environment. In the I-Hab → p. 118 design, the highly restricted space in the module made it necessary to create more space for daily activities, such as exercise, which was resolved through the design of retractable crew quarters.

Watching astronauts navigate through the interior of the space station, it becomes obvious that the logics that guide design on Earth often do not apply here. Architects are challenged to respond with smart solutions that support and potentially "re-ground" astronauts in an otherwise foreign environment.

Deep Space

We are right at the edge of our technology's ability to meet the challenges of outer space. Just keeping people alive in this environment is very, very hard. Once we have solved the fundamental problems over the next 50 years—life support, space radiation, mitigating the deconditioning of reduced gravity, and the psychological challenges—those very hard problems will cease to dominate. Then, as space settlements grow, much older, more familiar human issues will begin to take over. Eventually we will regard life support equipment and variable gravity and radiation shielding as facts of life for which we have routine, predictable solutions. Older challenges of how people interact and how people can be productive and fulfilled in their environment will drive how we design and build places for private, group, and public living and industry that enable space communities and culture and cities. The more traditional issues will take over again.

*Brent Sherwood, Senior Vice President
for Advanced Development Programs, Blue Origin
(Radio Orange Space Specials: Could we prevent people
from going to the Moon or Mars? 15 Aug 2006)*

Mars

Moon

Orbit

Earth Land
Earth Ocean

When you arrive in microgravity you do not have the same references anymore, it is not the same space anymore as it is when you train on the ground, it is crowded with stuff and it is totally different. It is a totally different volume, it is huge and you realise you live in a volume not in an area (plane).

Claudie Haignere, former French Astronaut and Politician
(The Human Perspective, Volume: Getting There, Being There, 2010, v25)

Replicating Terrestrial Systems

Natural life-supporting systems on Earth continue to exist largely unnoticed, revealed only when they are impacted to the point where environments fail to sustain life. Abnormalities such as a colour change in contaminated water or breathing difficulties as a result of air pollution may warn living beings of the potential toxicity of their environments via sensory cues.[1] Nuclear disasters, the aftermath of oil spills and forest fires may threaten living systems in the long term by compromising vital conditions of survival. Human survival is dependent on the life-supporting environmental conditions we are accustomed to on Earth; a continuous supply of uncontaminated air, water and food, and protection from harmful external impacts.

To sustain human life outside the Earth's atmosphere, natural systems from Earth need to be replicated. Living in outer space requires the creation of an artificial biosphere in its most minimal terms. Having sustained the life of more than 250 astronauts and cosmonauts for almost 25 years, the International Space Station (ISS) remains a prominent example of human presence—and survival—in outer space. Its interior hosts a complex, technological Environmental Control and Life Support System (ECLSS) that mimics familiar, life-sustaining factors such as the convection of breathable air, the recovery of water and the removal of noxious gases, trace contaminants and particulate matter from the air. The pressurised habitat modules are operated under standard terrestrial air pressure, with fans to circulate the interior air and keep a moderate temperature of around 20°C. Oxygen is generated and recovered on board by splitting oxygen from water via electrolysis, powered by solar panels. The remaining hydrogen is used in the Sabatier reaction to turn CO_2 into water and methane.[2] Water is recovered from urine, wastewater and humidity. As a safe-guarding measure against potential system failure, the system includes redundant backup systems such as pressurised oxygen tanks.

Ensuring contingency in these distant environments is essential as components may not be resupplied or manufactured in time. Remedial maintenance of a life support system (LSS) is undertaken when parts fail, malfunction or break; these can be impacted by technological failures, microbial growth or environmental changes. Both ground control and crew members continuously monitor the data provided by the ECLSS. To alert astronauts to changes in their environment the levels of oxygen, partial oxygen pressure, CO_2, radiation, fungal and bacterial growth, volatile organic compounds, humidity, temperature and noise are continuously monitored. NASA astronauts are provided with a Malfunction Procedure Manual to direct them in the circumstance of any predicted system failure.[3] Although not posing an immediate threat to the crew, slight air leakage on the space station is an ongoing issue and requires the search and sealing of microcracks formed due to material fatigue or the load stress of docking and undocking manoeuvres.

When outside of their spacecraft or space station an astronaut relies on a Portable Life Support System (PLSS) which is integrated into each individual spacesuit. These personal biospheres provide a pressurised environment for astronauts to breathe, urinate, hydrate and maintain a stable temperature. Different suits are designed to address different environmental contexts: Extra-Vehicular Activity (EVA), Intra-Vehicular Activity (IVA), microgravity → p. 131 or surface environments. Like the ECLSS on the International Space Station, the PLSS relies on a number of components to support the life of the astronaut. The suit itself is composed of many material layers, each with different functions for the protection or support of the wearer. Tubes that circulate water are woven into a garment to sustain suitable temperature levels inside the suit.[4] Hardware is attached to different parts of the suit. The LSS contained within the backpack of the suit holds and distributes oxygen, and filters out carbon dioxide. Space suit sensors track multiple parameters such as CO_2, oxygen, humidity, respiration, skin temperature, heart rate and blood oxygen levels. For a few hours, the EVA spacesuit is a wearable space habitat.

Long-term missions into deep space will require self-sufficiency involving LSS that mimic the fully circular conditions on Earth. Space habitats will be designed to fully recycle their waste products into water, oxygen, food and other substances. There have been a number of biosphere testbeds in preparation for outer space habitation such as: the Soviet BIOS-3 (1972-1984), Biosphere 2 in Arizona, USA (1990s) and the NASA Lunar-Mars Life Support Test Project (LMLSTP)[5] (1995 and 1997).[6] Each of them provided valuable insights regarding the limits and challenges of the design and engineering of closed ecosystems. LMLSTP, a retrofit of an existing 6 m long vacuum chamber based in the Johnson Space Center, housed astronauts for development and testing → p. 175 of LSS equipment.[7] One of the main takeaways from the retrofit was to develop and design internal configurations → p. 40 together with architects to incorporate human factors. Crew members' well-being and performance are directly influenced by decisions on lighting, colour, configuration and function; all of which are impacted by the arrangement of interior LSSs. Countermeasures against elevated noise levels produced by equipment or other team members are considered critical for crew performance and comfort. Developing a closed-loop system suitable for human habitation also relies on architects factoring in the well-being and performance of astronauts in design.

Reliable bioregenerative LSS, involving microbes and plant-based life are considered key for the success of long-term human missions in outer space. Biogenerative life support systems have been investigated in ESA's MELiSSA programme (Micro-Ecological Life Support System Alternative) for more than 30 years and are increasingly trialled in terrestrial architecture in order to address urban sustainability and resource management. The Living Architecture project

Living Architecture → p. 166

prototyped a selectively programmable bioreactor capable of water purification and generation of low-voltage electricity, oxygen and biomass, as well as the recovery of valuable substances such as phosphate, as a result of microbial activity. EDEN-ISS,

Eden – ISS → p. 146

a greenhouse and ground demonstration facility of plant cultivation technologies for safe food production in space, is another example of a bioregenerative LSS component. Both of these architectural scenarios incorporate living systems, one of them designed to be embedded in the structure of a building and the other to be established in the extreme environments of outer space. Future LSS, incorporating both physiochemical and bioregenerative systems, must act as an all-encompassing system capable of recycling waste back into usable resources.

LIQUIFER   Deep Space

                                                                         Mars

                                                                         Moon

                                                                         Orbit

                                                                         138
                                                                         Earth Land
                                                                         Earth Ocean

Earth

General characteristics

The abundance of surface water on Earth differentiates it from other planets in our solar system. More than 70 percent of the planetary surface of Earth is covered by oceans and large stretches of land are covered by vegetation. The topological features of the terrain above and below sea level are impacted by active tectonic movements, volcanic activity, erosion and the presence of biological systems.

The Earth's biosphere, the zone where life exists, constitutes a thin layer at the planetary surface, reaching from the ocean floor to several kilometres into the atmosphere. All life forms that feed on organic matter derive their energy from photosynthesising organisms capable of transforming inorganic matter into biomass by using sunlight as a source of energy. Human activity and an increasing global population have significantly affected the planet's biosphere. Today agriculture occupies half of the world's habitable land and its impacts are threatening the biosphere integrity.[1]

Atmosphere and magnetosphere

Earth orbits the Sun at a distance that allows the formation and persistence of liquid surface water, a prerequisite for life. Life on Earth is protected by the presence of a global magnetic field which is generated by the convective flow of molten iron-rich matter within the Earth's core. This global magnetosphere shields the planet against solar wind by deflecting and trapping solar particles in the Van Allen Belts, two torus-shaped belts around Earth, and thereby prevents the erosion of the climate-moderating atmosphere. Earth's original atmosphere contained large proportions of methane, ammonia and water vapour but no free oxygen.[2] The current presence of 21 percent oxygen is associated with the emergence of photosynthesising organisms that generate atmospheric oxygen as a by-product of their metabolism.

The atmosphere of Earth is defined in layers.[3] The lowest layer, the troposphere, extends from the Earth's surface to an average altitude of 12 km and contains nearly all atmospheric water vapour. It is characterised by rotational turbulence and dynamic weather phenomena that are influenced by temperature, humidity, surface topography and the Earth's axial rotation. The stratosphere sits above the troposphere extending to approximately 50 km in altitude. It holds the ozone layer, a protective layer which absorbs harmful UV radiation from the Sun. From 50 km to 85 km above sea level the mesosphere still contains sufficient gas to cause frictional heating of meteoroids, associated with the visual phenomena of shooting stars. The Kármán Line is the defined border between Earth and space, drawn at 100 kilometres above sea level.

Space exploration

Some deserts, polar regions or high-altitude regions show similarities with the environmental conditions of other planetary surfaces and have been acknowledged as analogue sites for space mission simulations → p. 175 to test and improve infrastructure and procedures.

Many notable technologies developed for space have been successfully transferred to large-scale applications on Earth and technologies developed on Earth provide solutions for space applications. Certain research fields such as biomimetics provide solutions for varied applications in outer space and on Earth by transferring principles from biological role models into technological solutions. Raising awareness of these shared benefits for both Earth and outer space supports ongoing investment for R&D in space exploration.

	Earth
Mean Surface Gravity	9.80 m/s²
Equatorial Diameter	12 756 km
Equatorial Circumference	40 030 km
Surface Pressure	1.014 bar
Length of Year	365 days
Length of Day	24 hours
Temperature Range	−89°C to +57°C

Deep Space

Mars

Moon

Orbit

LIQUIFER Projects on   Earth's Land
Earth Ocean

143—
173

In October 2017 the Eden – ISS Mobile Test Facility left from Bremen, Germany. Loaded onto the cargo ship, the Golden Karoo, in Hamburg it was shipped to Cape Town, South Africa.

The ship S.A. Agulhas II delivered the Eden – ISS facility to the Antarctic continent where it was unloaded at the sea ice edge on 3 January 2018.

Once transported to the mission site, 400 m from the Neumayer-Station III, the two containers were connected on a stationary platform.

Eden–ISS demonstrated on-Earth plant cultivation technologies for safe food production onboard the International Space Station (ISS) and for future human space exploration vehicles and planetary outposts. To advance innovative food cultivation technologies in closed-loop systems as an integral part of future space systems, the Mobile Test Facility (MTF) was conceived and installed in the extreme environment of Antarctica. The integral technologies of the project included: an advanced nutrient delivery system; high-performance LED lighting; a bio-detection and decontamination system; imaging systems for monitoring plant health; and robust thermal, power and air management systems.

During the Eden–ISS analogue mission, the MTF was deployed and tested in close proximity to the Neumayer III Antarctic station, operated by the Alfred Wegener Institute. In-situ, the MTF provided 270 kg of fresh, edible produce for the crew during the 2018 Antarctic winter. It continued to serve as an analogue environment for testing plant cultivation under extreme environmental and logistical conditions in Antarctica until 2021. Current plans suggest that the facility will be transferred to the Astronaut Centre of the European Space Agency.

LIQUIFER designed and outfitted the interior of the service section of the Eden–ISS facility. Coordinating the system requirements and the interfaces, the team also co-designed the space mission application of the greenhouse as a deployable greenhouse for the Moon and Mars. LIQUIFER was also responsible for project communication and dissemination activities.

T 2015–2019

P European Union – Horizon 2020 (EU-H2020) project, topic of space exploration & life support

C Consortium partners – German Aerospace Centre (DLR), Bremen, Germany; LIQUIFER Systems Group, Austria; National Research Council, Italy; University of Guelph, Canada; Alfred Wegener Institute for Polar and Marine Research, Germany; Enginsoft, Italy; Airbus Defence and Space, Germany; Thales Alenia Space, Italy; Aero Sekur, Italy; Wageningen University and Research, The Netherlands; Heliospectra, Sweden; Limerick Institute of Technology, Ireland; Telespazio, Italy

EDEN-ISS during the polar night which began at the end of May and ended in July. Outside temperatures dropped below -42 °C.

Such low temperatures created challenges for the greenhouse system and the DLR scientist, Paul Zabel, tasked with maintaining it and harvesting the plants.

All acquired data and imagery related to plant growth and systems operation were transmitted to the Mission Control Centre at DLR in Bremen for remote oversight.

Earth Land Project # Eden – ISS Prototype 149

Prior to the test campaign in Antarctica, the Eden – ISS systems were assembled, integrated and tested at DLR premises in Bremen.

The plant cultivation racks were fitted with a highly reliable illumination system which can be adapted to the specific light requirements of the selected crops.

The aeroponic irrigation technique uses a mist environment within the light protected root zone of the plant growth trays.

Early plant growth was supported by 3D-printed structures. Over 20 plant varieties were cultivated including lettuce, cucumber, radishes, dwarf tomatoes and strawberries.

The Mobile Test Facility was preinstalled at the premises of DLR Bremen. It consists of two main sections: the greenhouse and the service section.

Earth Land   Project   # Eden–ISS   Prototype

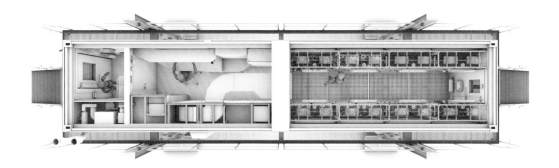

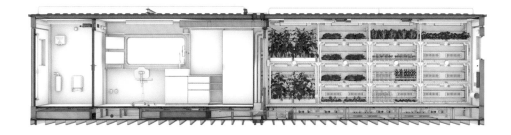

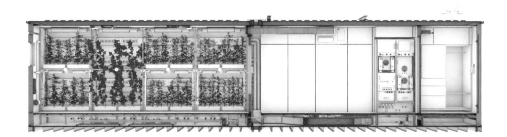

The service section houses all supply and control systems, a laboratory and the RUCOLA System, an experiment for plant growth on board the International Space Station (ISS).

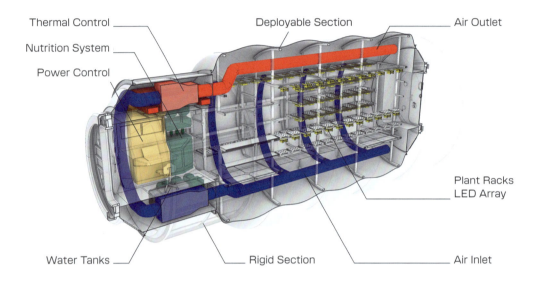

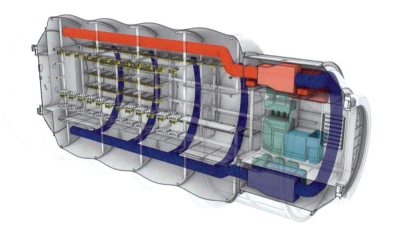

The project EDEN-ISS provided key findings regarding systems performance, crop yield, crew acceptance, and contamination for the design of a future greenhouse on the Moon or Mars.

Bio-regenerative Life Support System are a high priority requirement to meet the physical and psychological challenges of long-duration human space exploration.

Earth Land — Project Eden–ISS — Prototype

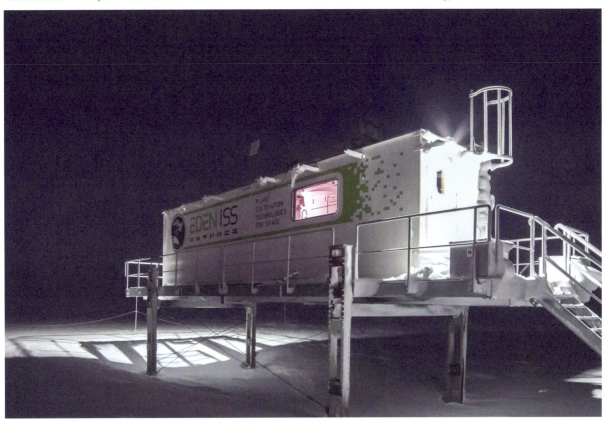

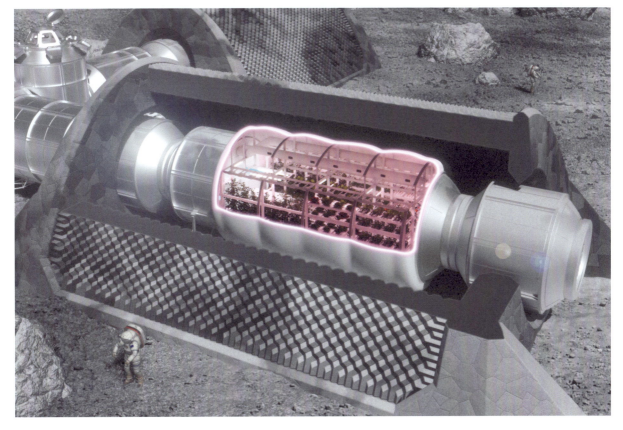

Closed-loop systems that consider the complementary nature of resource exchange within the metabolic processes of biological systems redefine waste as a valuable resource.

GrAB was an artistic research project that investigated growth patterns and dynamics in nature and applied them to architecture with the goal of creating a new living architecture. An interdisciplinary team from the fields of architecture, biology, art, mechatronics and robotics collaborated in the project. Selected biological processes were explored in depth to identify principles of growth and translate them into exemplary architectural visions. The project nurtured visions that merge alternative building techniques with biology and technology to increase the sustainability and resilience of urban architecture in the future. Principles from biology such as self-organisation, adaptivity and circularity were transferred into artistic concepts. Mobile 3D printing technologies were developed further and employed to produce these differentiated and adaptive structures.

With the support of the host institution, the University of Applied Arts Vienna, LIQUIFER conceived the project with architect Petra Gruber, led the research group and were co-principal investigators of GrAB. The team organised a three-year series of workshops and symposia, disseminating the findings in the book *Built to Grow* and an exhibition at the Angewandte Interdisciplinary Lab (AIL).

T 2013 – 2016

P Research project funded by the Austrian Science Fund (FWF) as part of PEEK 2012

C Collaborating institutions – University of Applied Arts, Vienna, Austria; Biomimetics & Mechanical Engineering Group, University of Bath, UK; Botanical Garden & Plant Biomechanics Group, University of Freiburg, Germany; Multi Actor Systems Department, Delft University of Technology, The Netherlands; Ethiopian Institute of Architecture, Building Construction and City Development, Addis Ababa University, Ethiopia; transarch office for biomimetics and transdisciplinary architecture, Austria

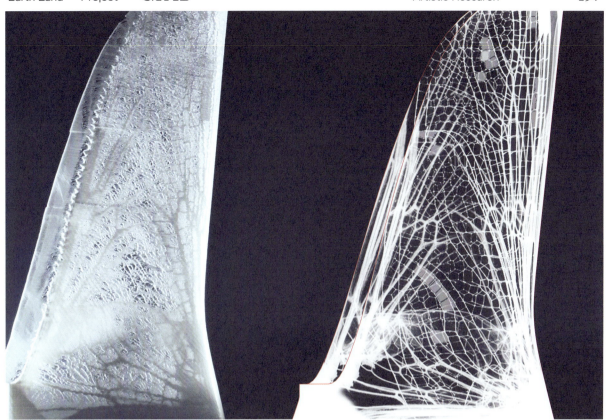
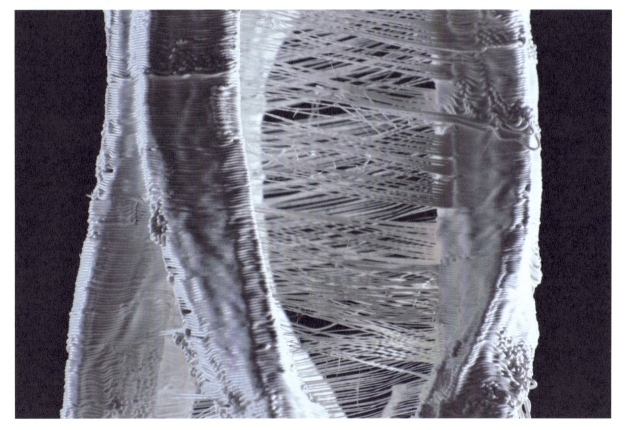

3D printing is an effective technology to mimic differentiations inherent to natural structures.

Mobile wire printers provide flexibility in transport and deployment. They can work interactively with the existing environment and react to previous building processes.

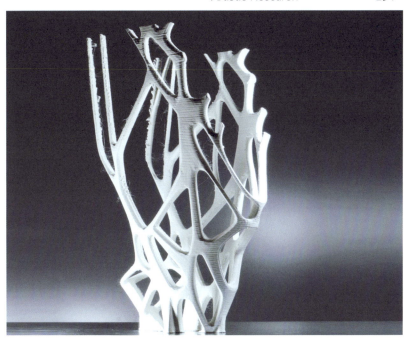

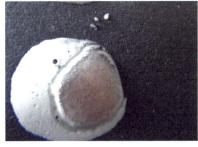

Additive manufacturing is complemented by subtractive methods that apply dissolving agents to the previously printed structure.

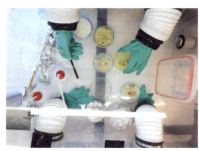 

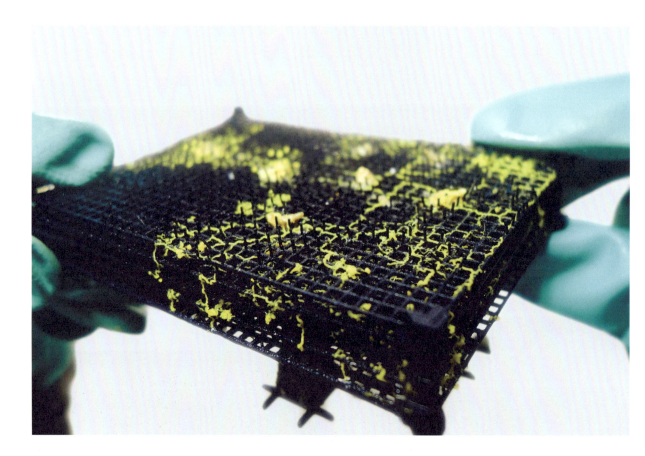

The explorative growth of slime mould within 3D printed structures was integrated into the architectural design process as a method of co-design.

Hands-on experiments are a highly effective way to gain valuable insights into the dynamics and vulnerabilities of living systems.

A range of biodegradable support structures were explored to generate shapes of higher complexity than the orthogonal mycelium brick.

Photosynthesizing microorganisms grow within a transparent tubular system when exposed to adequate lighting. Fish are incorporated to add to system robustness.

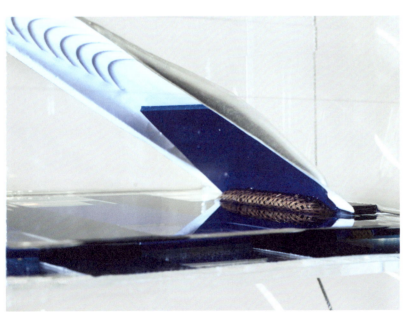

In correspondence to the cellular expansion growth principle, the characteristics of hydrogels (increasing in volume through water uptake) was used for the actuation of kinetic structures.

Earth Land   Project   # Living Architecture   Technology Development   165

Employing biological processes within a Living
Architecture will reduce the ecological impact
of the built environment through the establishment
of closed-loop systems.

Living Architecture provided the proof-of-concept for a next-generation, selectively programmable bioreactor technology that is envisioned as an integral component of human dwellings in the future, capable of complementing or replacing existing building services. At its core, the Living Architecture system processes waste streams in situ within a set of modular bioreactor building blocks that can be stacked to form a freestanding partition wall. The system merges three complementary technologies: the Microbial Fuel Cell (MFC) that purifies wastewater and produces electricity, the Photobioreactor (PBR) that generates oxygen and supplies nutrients for the Synthetic Microbial Consortia (SMC) that recovers valuable substances from the waste streams. With its circular approach, the Living Architecture technologies represent a step towards urban sustainability and responsible resource management.

As part of the Living Architecture team, LIQUIFER was responsible for scenario development and elaborated use cases for new and existing buildings, with customised solutions for different building types. The concepts were complemented by solar energy harvesting and vertical farming infrastructure. An immersive animation showcased the integrated systems within a multifunctional highrise building. As part of the building block design, LIQUIFER designed and built a brick prototype and produced a wide range of ceramic bioreactor membranes to selectively control the interaction across bioreactor chambers.

T 2016 – 2019

P European Union – Horizon 2020 (EU-H2020) research project, FET-Open

C Consortium partners – School of Architecture, Planning and Landscape & Institute for Sustainability, Newcastle University, UK; Unconventional Computing Centre, Department of Computer Science, Faculty of Environment and Technology, University of the West of England, UK; BioEnergy Centre, UK; Bristol Robotics Lab, UK; The Biological Research Centre, Department of Environmental Biology, Spanish National Research Council (CSIC), Spain; LIQUIFER Systems Group, Austria; EXPLORA BIOTECH, Italy; Centre for Integrative Biology, University of Trento, Italy

Earth Land   Project   **Living Architecture**   Technology Development   167

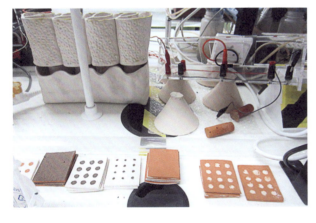

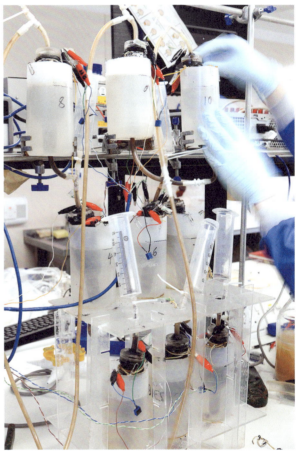

Ceramic membranes, an integral component of the bioreactor, were investigated through material, shape and surface variations.

Preliminary test set-ups explored the performance of alternative ceramic membranes with a focus on energy output or selective permeability.

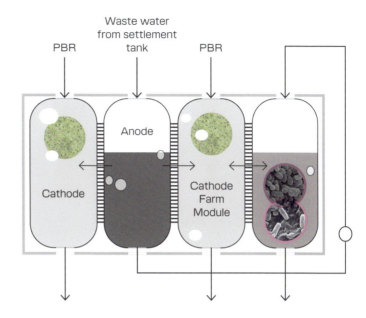

The activities of living organisms complement each other in the Living Architecture brick where three technologies are merged. In the Microbial Fuel Cell (MFC) technology microbes act as catalysts for electrochemical reactions within the anode and cathode system to purify wastewater and generate an electric current.

The photosynthesizing microbes used in the photobioreactor (PBR) technology are fed into the cathode chamber. A Farm Module is simultaneously part of the third technology using synthetic microbial consortia for the recovery of phosphate in the Labour Module.

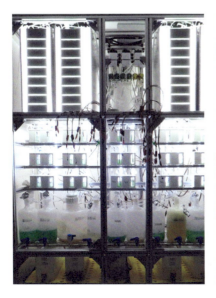
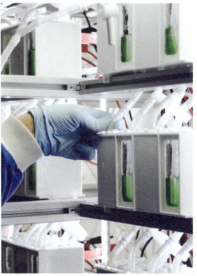

The proof-of-concept was demonstrated under laboratory conditions with a series of 3D printed four-chamber bricks.

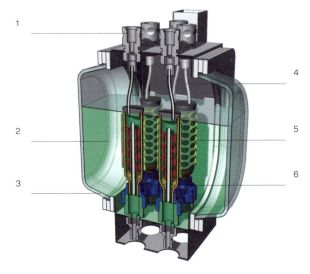

1 Hydraulic plug-in connectors
2 Combined photobioreactor, cathode and farm chamber
3 Removable glass window
4 Overflow systems
5 Cylindric ceramic membrane
6 Exchangeable cylindric anode or labour chamber

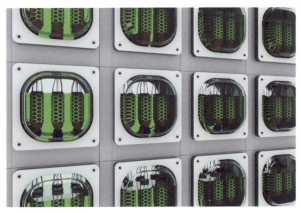

The LIQUIFER brick concept used cylindric anode and labour chambers immersed in a single volume that serves as photobioreactor, cathode and farm module.

The soft green glow of the bioreactor wall makes the metabolic processes visible within the building.

Earth Land   Project   Living Architecture   Technology Development   172

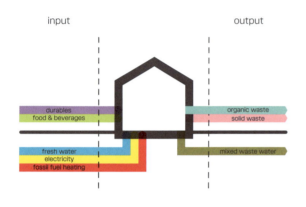

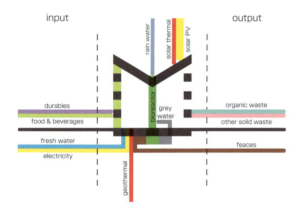

In combination with other renewable technologies, the Living Architecture system has the potential to drastically reduce the existing supply dependencies of the built environment.

Architectural scenarios explored the application of diverse and decentralised resource management for sustainable urban living.

Living Architecture

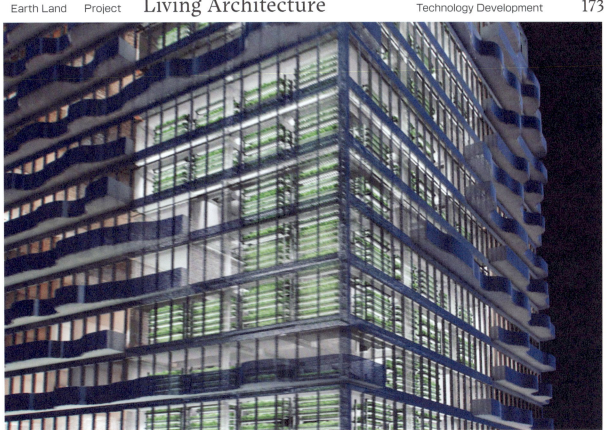

The integration of bioreactor walls within a multifunctional highrise building was showcased in an immersive animation.

Mars

Moon

Orbit

Earth Land
Earth Ocean

Mission Preparation: Simulating Future Explorations

After 110 days, four volunteer students exited the Lunar Palace 1, a bio-regenerative life support facility built to simulate a Lunar base at Beihang University, Beijing. The isolation experiment was the third stage of a 370-day simulation, which aimed to enable the coexistence of humans, animals, plants and microorganisms in an almost closed-loop environment.[1] Lunar Palace 1 was a successful example of a simulation capable of supporting biological chains for an extended duration in a closed environment Lunar base. The approximately 160 m² architecture, integrating the Bio-regenerative Life Support System (BLSS), → p. 135 was composed of three cabins, two of which were solely dedicated to the planting and harvesting of grain, vegetables and fruit.[2] The survival, and ultimate thriving, of individual organisms was dependent on the survival of the others: oxygen generated by plants became breathing air for the volunteers; carbon dioxide from the volunteers was utilised in the photosynthesis of plants; scraps from harvested grain, vegetables and fruit fed mealworms; other byproducts were treated before being used to fertilise plants. The Lunar-like environment was developed to test the design and operation of the BLSS as well as the physiological, social and psychological effects of long-term, closed-quarters isolation on volunteers.[3] As with most mission simulations, Lunar Palace 1 trained multiple skills including complex scenarios (planting, processing and harvesting food), understanding operations (abiding by the needs of the BLSS) and understanding the mission in relation to other crew members (working together to keep the BLSS functioning).

Simulations are a prerequisite phase for all planned missions to space. With limited actual experience in a space environment and the characteristic difficulties it offers, extensive preparation is necessary to minimise potential risks. Earth-based simulations provide researchers with an environment to observe, test and analyse their developments before they are utilised in actual space missions.[4] They can be approached as integrated space mission scenarios, as in the case of Lunar Palace 1, or they may investigate specific research questions in the fields of physics, geology, sociology, psychology or others. Like a rehearsal on a 1:1 scale, simulations follow mission-specific procedures, act out these guidelines, evaluate test setups, find solutions to problems and generate new knowledge. As each simulation is part of an iterative process, the findings fuel scientific, technological, design and procedural improvements. Results from simulations can help to train and test for future simulations and space missions.

Lunar Palace 1 took place in a highly controlled, artificial environment, similar to those developed by governmental space agencies and private enterprises for astronaut training. In addition, natural space analogues are frequently used to perform complex mission scenarios under conditions similar to the proposed space environment. Some extreme environments on Earth are recognised space analogue sites as they represent certain characteristics of the Lunar, Martian or orbital environments relevant to the objective of the simulation. Among others, this includes Arctic locations such as the Haughton impact crater on Devon Island, Canada, which is used to approximate the Martian environment due to its geology and frozen, desert-like landscape. The Atacama Desert, Chile and Rio Tinto, Spain are used as Mars mission analogue sites due to their extremely dry terrains, their pronounced mineral content and the types of microbial ecosystems able to survive in their extreme environments.[5] Underwater environments such as the Aquarius underwater analogue in Florida are used to simulate different gravity levels when performing various EVA scenarios.

All mission simulations have an objective. Some simulations have broad objectives, such as the project Moonwalk, which aimed to enhance European capabilities for future human space exploration, especially surface Extra-Vehicular Activity (EVA) for the Moon and Mars.[6] For others, there are more specific objectives, as in FASTER, which aimed to develop technologies allowing rovers to safely and efficiently traverse other-planetary terrain.[7] As a less complex simulation with fewer variables, it was possible to test FASTER inside the Airbus DS Mars Yard Facility in Stevenage, England, a purpose-built enclosed site. This type of testing is cheaper and more common than integrated mission simulations such as Moonwalk, which test multiple elements at once. Moonwalk required two space analogue sites: Rio Tinto, Spain and subsea Marseille, France, plus a mission control connected to both

Moonwalk → p. 188

FASTER → p. 74

sites, which was located near Brussels, Belgium. This simulation took place over two weeks, where an astronaut and assistant rover collaborated as partners in mapping, surveying and sampling activities. It tested technical components developed by the seven Moonwalk partners, such as the small assistant robot, the EVA simulation spacesuit, and the EVA information system, in addition to a mission control centre, a biomonitoring system and a set of manual tools for EVA.[8] A series of mission scenarios were designed to test these novel technologies and tools, incorporating procedures similar to those that astronauts use on the International Space Station (ISS). Like a storyboard for a film, mission scenarios sketch the proposed sequence of scenes for each scenario. The "actors" (astronaut and rover) were then able to rehearse a series of actions inside the relevant environment and given timeframes. In repeating these tasks, concepts and technologies that the team had developed could be analysed and evaluated. Scenarios included scouting a site, collecting soil samples, exploring a cave, exploring challenging terrain and exploring a steep slope. The simulation replicated conditions that would be encountered in the Martian environment, including time delay in communicating with Earth-based teams.

In addition to these physical spaces, virtual reality technologies are being utilised to create simulation "locations." As technology advances, Space Architects can simulate and test their designs with astronauts before constructing a physical prototype. In the case of

I-Hab → p. 118

I-Hab interior design development (a part of the future Lunar Orbital Space Station Gateway), LIQUIFER had the opportunity to interact and receive feedback from ESA astronauts that prime contractor Thales Alenia Space Italy (TAS-I) invited to explore the rendered 48 m³ configuration of the proposed interior layout. In order to design suitable, feasible habitats, simulations are an essential component in preparing for the challenges proposed by future space missions.

By practising simulations, astronauts learn not only what to do during their mission by heart but also rehearse for being in outer space—working and acting as if they are already at their mission destination off-Earth. This familiarising of the strange helps them feel more comfortable when being in actual harsh environments, where errors can have deadly consequences.

Joseph Popper, artist and designer
(Radio Orange Space Specials: Exploring the Peripheries of Outer Space, 18 Oct 2020)

A simulator is basically the same structure as the real vehicle used in spaceflight in Russian programs because you need to test the hardware. The main difference is the real vehicle flies. We built several samples of vehicles based on the same drawing. Using one of these mock-ups, we basically tried to break it. Usually, after all these tests it became the simulator.

Sergei Krikalev, Soviet and Russian mechanical engineer and former cosmonaut
(Radio Orange Space Specials: Long duration stays on space stations, 19 Aug 2008)

Deep Space

Simulations allow us to spot the unknown—those elements you couldn't predict and issues that you didn't foresee. You learn from them and optimise them as they allow you to address these sticking points. You need to progressively prepare on Earth so that when the time to do it comes, you are ready. That's the main thing.

Diego Urbina, Team Leader, Future Projects and Exploration, Space Applications Services
(Radio Orange Space Specials: Simulations:
space exploration preparations on Earth, 19 Jul 2016)

Mars

Moon

Orbit

Earth Land
Earth Ocean

In chamber studies you cannot simulate risks to life and health. These two factors, which are common dangers of spaceflight, exist in Antarctica. The point is, no analogue can be perfect for spaceflight, so we need to distribute the experience in various analogues like submarines, oil platforms, Antarctica and arctic winter.

Vadim Gushin, Psychologist for Russian Cosmonauts
(Radio Orange Space Specials: Psychology in Space, 28 Dec 2010)

LIQUIFER   Deep Space

                                                                            Mars

                                                                            Moon

                                                                            Orbit

                                                                         Earth Land
                                                                         Earth Ocean
                                                                         180

Underwater

General characteristics

Liquid water is essential to life. It is a universal solvent and transport medium of energy and matter on multiple scales. Within oceans, water streams and in the bodies of living organisms water transmits nutrients and waste and regulates both temperature and internal cellular pressure.

Underwater, light and sound travel and disperse differently than they do in air. In water, sound waves propagate much faster than in air.[1] Its reflection and absorption of light depend on surface characteristics and the particles present in the water. Water scatters light and absorbs various wavelengths differently, orange/red light can penetrate less deep than blue light, making deep, clear ocean water appear blue. Marine life is supported by solar radiation, which warms the oceanic surface, and supplies energy to photosynthetic microorganisms and phytoplankton which live in the well-lit surface waters of the euphotic zone.[2] Water can shield organisms from harmful cosmic radiation, a characteristic that promoted the evolution of early lifeforms on Earth.

Hydrosphere

The hydrosphere is the total mass of water on planet Earth including that in a liquid, gaseous and frozen state. Freshwater accounts for a very small share of the global water volume, whilst more than 97 percent is accounted for by saline water.[3] Large volumes of fluids, atmospheric gases and oceanic water are important factors for global heat storage and redistribution. The hydrologic cycle is the redistribution of water by evaporation, condensation, precipitation, transpiration and run-off. Oceanic water circulates globally because of density differences directly related to variations in temperatures and salinity. While surface currents in oceans are affected by planetary rotation and wind, deep oceanic water currents are determined by deep sea and coastal topography. Massive vertical movements of ocean water happen in specific deep convection areas close to the poles where water sinks with increasing density and upwells in equatorial regions.[4] Ocean surface topography maps the highs and lows of the ocean surface affected by weather phenomena and the Moon's gravitational pull on Earth. Seabed topography maps depth contours, oceanic plateaus, plains and basins, subsea volcanoes, banks, ridges and trenches.

Space exploration

Underwater environments are used as testbeds for space exploration missions to simulate → p. 175 reduced gravity → p. 131 environments. Simulation suits are designed to provide variable levels of buoyancy when simulating operations for reduced gravity or microgravity. Simulations are undertaken either in laboratory settings such as the Neutral Buoyancy Laboratory at the Johnson Space Centre or in large bodies of water, often oceans. In simulated microgravity, astronauts learn to no longer rely on their weight, but to move and reposition via propulsive or pulling forces. Underwater training can only approximate the experience of reduced gravity because the movement through water produces considerable drag compared to movement in a vacuum or air.[5] Underwater environments are also used to simulate extended periods of isolation. The operational similarities and living conditions in submarines can be compared to life in space habitats, in terms of the lack of space, lack of resources and extreme pressure differences between the interior and exterior of the vessel.

Underwater

Gravity	simulation by buoyancy variation
Average Salinity	~35 g/L
Euphotic Zone range	from surface up to 200 m (clear water)
Pressure increase with depth	1 bar / 10 m
Speed of Sound	approx. 1500 (water) 340 (air) m.s^{-1}
Surface Temperature Range	−2 to +35 °C

Deep Space

Mars

Moon

Orbit

Earth Land
LIQUIFER Projects in Earth's Ocean
**185—
195**

Moonwalk developed scenarios and technologies for human-robot cooperation at planetary surface missions and tested the performance of an astronaut-robot team at two analogue sites on Earth, in Rio Tinto, Spain →p. 64 and Marseille, France. Simulation astronauts (simonauts) were supported by a small mobile assistant robot during extravehicular activities (EVA). To simulate partial gravity conditions on the Moon, the astronaut-robot team was tested in underwater environments in Marseilles, at first in a controllable testing pool and subsequently in a natural subsea environment.

Underwater simulations entail additional requirements for hardware operability and safety standards, when compared to on-ground simulations →p. 64. The rover, spacesuits and tools designed have to be adapted to a level of buoyancy that simulates partial gravity. Divers' equipment is integrated into the spacesuit to sustain extended periods underwater. For safety reasons, each simonaut is accompanied and surveilled by security divers. In natural subsea environments, the additional requirements of an adequately equipped ship and its crew substantially impact simulation costs. Visibility in a natural subsea environment can be reduced as a result of natural turbulence related to weathering and currents.

Apart from the development of mission scenarios, the LIQUIFER team designed an exchangeable payload system for the rover chassis and several astronaut tools. The design included casings for measuring instruments, sample storage and tool fittings on the rover, as well as expandable and collapsible tools for the astronaut that reflect the restrictions of movement and visibility when wearing a heavy and bulky EVA suit. LIQUIFER were also responsible for the communication and dissemination of the project.

T   2013 – 2016

P   European Union – Seventh Framework Programme for Research and Technological Development (EU-FP7), in the frame of space

C   Consortium partners – DFKI Robotics Innovation Center, Germany; COMEX, France; EADS UK, UK; LIQUIFER Systems Group, Austria; Space Applications Services, Belgium; NTNU Centre for Interdisciplinary Research in Space, Norway; INTA Instituto Nacional de Técnica Aeroespacial, Spain

L   Marseilles, France

Earth Ocean   Project   # Moonwalk   Prototype

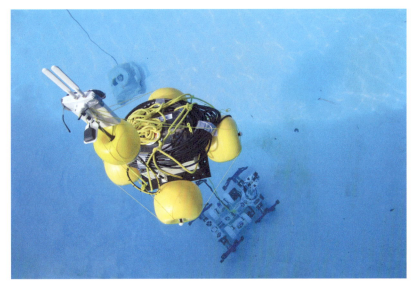

The underwater environment allows the testing of space exploration scenarios under simulated low-gravity conditions.

Pool tests at the COMEX premises in Marseille preceded the simulations in natural underwater environment, both involved a lander mock-up fragment equipped with a suitport, two simulation spacesuits and a robotic rover.

A simonaut accesses the Gandolfi 2 EVA simulation spacesuit through the suitport of the lander mockup and descends to the simulated Lunar surface.

Moonwalk

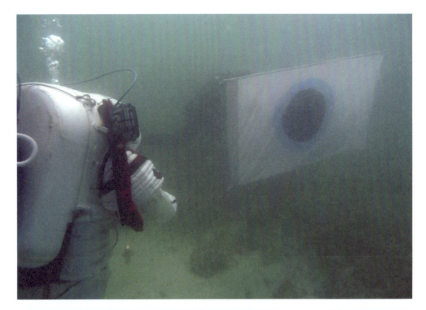

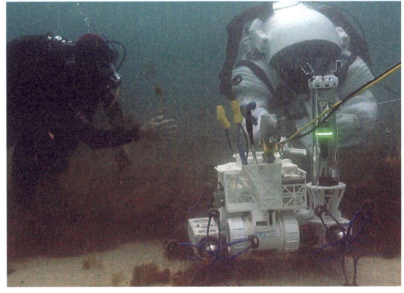

The next generation of space explorers contributed their ideas in the Moonwalk childrens' competition. The winning entry for the Moon flag design was honoured during the subsea simulation.

Simulations in natural subsea environments involve up to five security divers and several sea-going vessels.

Earth Ocean   Project   Moonwalk   Prototype   192

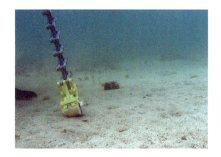

In accordance with the Mars simulations carried out in Rio Tinto, Spain, the underwater simulations studied and compared the performance of an astronaut-robot team with an astronaut-astronaut team.

The properties of the simulation spacesuits, the robotic rover and the sampling tools, were adapted for underwater applications to simulate Lunar gravity conditions.

The Medusa project explores the feasibility of inflatable habitats for use on planetary surfaces such as the Moon or Mars. The simulation →p. 64 concept involves a fully submerged habitat module that is anchored to the seafloor. It consists of a rigid core element that contains life support systems →p. 135, EVA infrastructure for entrance and exit from below and the surrounding torus-shaped living space. Internal vehicular activity (IVA) and EVA can be tested and validated within and outside the Medusa habitat. The segmented habitat hull was conceived as a membrane cushion structure which can perform various functions. Transparent structural segments serve as windows or as algae pods for producing nutrition supplements. For space applications, all hull membrane segments would be filled with water to provide radiation shielding for the crew. For the underwater simulation, LIQUIFER explored different testing possibilities. The hull segments could be filled with water around an inflated interior space or, in an alternative configuration, partial gravity can be simulated within a water-filled interior space surrounded by inflated hull segments.

LIQUIFER designed the Medusa deployable habitat in cooperation with subsea engineers from French engineering firm COMEX as well as developing the bioreactor concept with artist, biologist and space systems researcher Angelo Vermeulen.

T   2012
P   Concept design for a competition entry to the Jacques Rougerie Foundation
C   Collaborating partners – COMEX, France; LIQUIFER Systems Group, Austria, Delft University of Technology, The Netherlands

Earth Ocean   Project   *Medusa*   Prototype

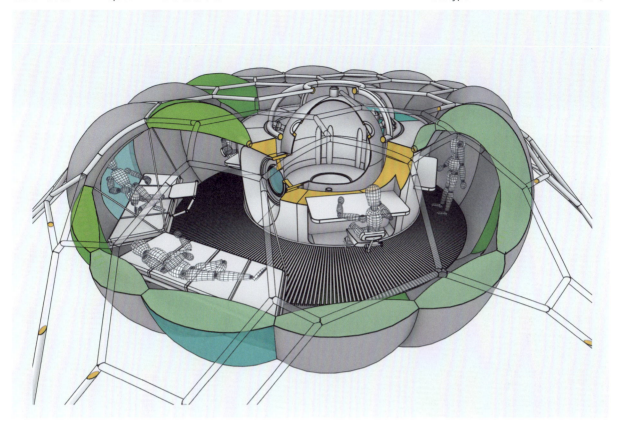

Working and living happens in the open space that surrounds a rigid core element acting as the entry point of the habitat.

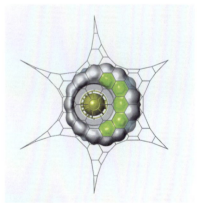

Underwater simulation for an outpost on the Martian surface.

The 1st Antarctic Biennale began in Ushuaia, Argentina, the southernmost city of our planet. During landings at scientific bases and historic and natural sites in the Antarctic Peninsula artists made temporary, site-specific and ecologically compatible installations and performances.

The following conversation is made up of selected interview segments from the podcast mini-series Antarctic Biennale by Barbara Imhof.

T — March 2017

P — Biennale commissioned and curated by artist Alexander Ponomarev, and curated by Nadim Samman

A — Artists – Alexander Ponomarev, Russia; Abdullah al Saadi, UAE; Alexis Anastasio, Brazil; Andrey Kuzkin, Russia; Gustav Düsing, Germany; Joaquin Fargas, Argentina; Julian Charrière, France/Switzerland; Juliana Cerqueira Leite, Brazil; Julius von Bismarck, Germany; Paul Rosero Contreras, Ecuador; Sho Hasegawa, Japan; Tomas Saraceno, Argentina/Germany; Zhang Enli, China; Yto Barrada, Morocco/France; Eulalia Valldosera, Spain; Shama Rahman, Bangladesh/UK; Yasuaki Igarashi, Japan; Lou Sheppard, Canada

I — Interdisciplinary Partners – Alexander Sekatskii, Russia; Barbara Imhof, Austria; Jean de Pomereu, France; Listen Schultz, Sweden; Carlo Rizzo, Italy/UK; Wakana Kono, Japan; Sergey Pisarev, Russia; Susmita Mohanty, Indian; Hector Monslave, Argentina; Adrian Dannatt, UK; Miguel Petchkovsky, Angola/Portugal; Liz Barry, USA; Nicholas Shapiro, USA

Antarctic Biennale

Adrian Dannatt Never before have I taken a journey in my life of 12 hours or 24 hours with no change in the landscape around, where nothing changes that I'm looking at.

Dehlia Hannah I've had an obsession about coming here for at least the last few years, ever since I've been doing my post-doctoral research on climate change aesthetics. I actually had a dream to get aboard a scientific mission to Antarctica.

Nadim Samman Antarctica is a place that is communicated as being central to our understanding of planetary systems, such as climate change, or the geophysical sciences. It's a place that everyone is told about, a place that everyone is expected to care about, a place that grabs the imagination that seems both otherworldly and intensely connected to everything else on this planet. Antarctica is so central to many of our contemporary narratives. And yet, most people will never go. We choose to go here in order to find a way to communicate, perhaps an undiscovered aspect of Antarctica's cultural potential. We do that with artists and philosophers and thinkers in the hope that they may find a way to interpret Antarctica anew.

Juliana Cerqueira Leite Just observing the forms that the ice makes and the icebergs that we've gone by, and these glaciers coming down mountains that are just the accumulation of snow. To me there's this process of sedimentation, of compression, of collapse, that is repeated in these shapes that we keep seeing, which I don't think is a normal thing to see. I've been finding it's very much a kind of visual signature of this environment.

Jean de Pomereau What we found out is that even what we thought was the most remote and the most detached of places is actually deeply relevant, it is all interdependent. And, what's more, there is a great pleasure to be drawn from that. It's both a place which delights and brings strong emotions of wonder, and at the same time, frightens us in its ability to echo across the world and across climatic issues.

Annex   Exploration   Deep Sea Minding

This expedition to the islands of Tonga in the South Pacific was part of the transdisciplinary research project Deep Sea Minding, which proposed the creation of structures that could serve the needs and desires of both humans and marine creatures.

The following conversation is made up of selected interview segments from the podcast mini-series *Deep Sea Minding* by Barbara Imhof.

T   Summer 2018

P   Summer 2018, expedition commissioned by TBA21–Academy, conceived by the Danish artist group SUPERFLEX

C   Collaborators — SUPERFLEX (Jakob Fenger, Bjørnstjerne Christiansen and Rasmus Nielsen); Francesca Thyssen-Bornemisza & Markus Reymann, TBA21-Academy; Dayne Buddo, Alligator Head Foundation; Ricardo Gomes, KWY.studio; Barbara Imhof, LIQUIFER Systems Group; Alex Jordan, Max Planck Institute Department of Collective Behaviour; Jun Kamei, AMPHIBIO; Maureen Penjueli, Pacific Network on Globalization; Johan Schneévoigt, cinematographer and cameraman

Deep Sea Minding

Rasmus Nielsen   The project is called Deep Sea Minding. That sounds a little bit like deep sea mining, which is a new mining adventure that is about to take off, where giant machines will start digging into the oceans, for various minerals and metals, because we are supposedly running out of them on land. There is a lot of concern about drilling on the seabed, we know that mining will be or has been disastrous in some parts of the world. So we thought, it would be nice to think of the deep sea as something else that is not a "gold hunt" for minerals, metals and things like that, but rather a "gold hunt" for ideas. So basically, try and imagine that you could learn something from the deep sea, that might influence life on land.

Francesca Thyssen-Bornemisza   Deep Sea Minding suggests dealing with the ocean, in its volume. We tend to look at the ocean as a surface.

Maureen Penjueli   The gravity of the significance of the ocean to life itself is quite significant.

Markus Reymann   When you try to think *from* the ocean, which is a very hard exercise, then you understand that everything is constantly changing. Everything is constantly in movement, everything is constantly in flux. And every action has a reaction and it's pretty visible.

Alex Jordan   I would love to erase or blur that line between the surface world and the deep. Not physically but in terms of intellectual engagement and to have people think about these very questions. What does that world require? What is good in that world?

Bjørnstjerne Christiansen   We wanted to explore the infrastructural relations between above and below, and how humans and sea organisms can interact and live together.

Jakob Fenger   Maybe one solution is to actually do a coexistence of some sort. More people have been to the Moon than to the deepest part of the ocean, it is really an unknown territory.

Ricardo Gomes   Any structure under the water has to allow water to flow through it and also to provide small and large spaces for different species, and their different types of behaviour. So fish may want to interact with the structure at a quantum playing level but most of the time when fish use structures, they do so to hide from predators. Whereas coral or algae will need space that is protected. The initial process was research in terms of what type of structures do fish or other marine life inhabit, or what type of structure do they create for themselves, which is actually quite rare. There's only very few species that actively interact with structures underwater that have been built.

Dayne Buddo   We find that we have to intervene, on an ecological basis, to make sure that we actually are doing the right things to enhance the environment and not degrade the environment by our actions. You can design structures that will actually enhance the marine environment and ecosystem resilience.

The Space–Earth Continuum

Epilogue
by Christina Ciardullo

Surrounded by a vast sea of darkness, there it is: that pale blue dot carrying everything that ever lived.[1] Just the right distance, just the right temperature, just the right mix of chemicals, at just the right time, to sustain life as we know it. For a very brief moment in the epic scale of space and time, we see evidence of something changing, something breathing, something metabolising, something regulating an atmosphere:[2] for a very brief moment, we exist.

There was a change the moment we saw the Earth from space. That distant view put in perspective just how lucky we are, collectively. It provoked a global evolution of consciousness that decades later can be recognised as a catalyst for some of our most recent environmental movements. And now, for perhaps the first time in more recent industrial and extractive history, there is mass mobilisation towards reconciling the needs of humans with that of our home planet. When we see the Earth from space, we become aware of how critically we are interdependent with our environment. It is the site of the evolution of our bodies. Our physical attributes, our attitudes, our fears and hopes are all a result of an evolutionary dialogue with our environment over hundreds of thousands of years. The way we build is also a reaction to the environment: the climate determines our standards, preconceptions, cultures, histories, geographies, climates, tools and materials. That unlikely chemical mix in time and space, somehow created the conditions for the very particular ways in which we live and create our built environments.

In the past half century heroic efforts have created *Enclosures* (spaceships) to preserve ourselves away from Earth. We have created *Architecture* for outer space. In outer space, architecture will act as a surrogate for our entire planet. A bubble of air and material will be the basis of a *Building,* substituting all the chemical and biological interactions that sustain us on Earth. Rather than conceive of spaceships and habitats as we do buildings on Earth, design for space allows us to remove our assumptions about what we think we know and instead work from a place where natural and social sciences meet design. This new perspective on architecture is not meant for space habitats alone. Now, as we contemplate new space stations and Lunar and Martian settlements, the UN predicts that 68 percent of the world's population will be living in cities. As it stands, maintaining the status quo within building and construction impacts the human condition in today's "developed" world: the majority of people spend 87 percent of their time *inside* buildings,[3] buildings which account for 35 percent of the global energy use and 38 percent of global carbon emissions.[4] On Earth we are still faced with immense scales of material extraction, global manufacturing chains, and energy production which contribute to global climate change and pollution. As the figures prove, the production of buildings is one of the biggest contributors to this fraught reality due to current, outdated approaches to material use, construction and design.

With a number of colleagues we determined that "any experience in creating and demonstrating a human environment that operates within limited means and resources at scale will have immense promise to return knowledge and provide feedback for buildings on Earth."[5] It is clear that there remains such dissonance between the way we propose to build on the Moon, Mars or further into our universe and the abandon with which we construct "modern" buildings on Earth. We must recognise and begin to act as though materials, energy, physical space, and resources are limited. To do so we must understand that the problems of the built environment in any location are both systemic and interconnected:

Physical Space

Meeting the demands of affordable housing for a rising population is predicted to double the amount of constructed floorspace by 2060. In more "developed" countries the amount of living space per person has doubled due to ageing populations, more people living alone and increases in standards of living. Building more means using more land, more materials, more energy, and more resources. Many have advocated for a shift in consciousness in relation to expectations of space and spaces. In this scenario, individual footprints would be reduced by living in smaller spaces and adapting spaces for multifunctionality or time-sharing.

Astronauts have so far lived in tight quarters, and as long as journeys are brief we can tolerate living small. But, as we design for longer and farther stays off Earth we must balance size and resource use with psychological and social health. It is not about living ascetically but about living well and fully within limited means: a task the designs you see from LIQUIFER have deftly mastered in spades.→ p. 52, 122 Designing for smaller and smarter spaces is not only key to our future on Earth, it is the essential role of the architect in space.

Resources
Nothing is closer to the human body than water, air, and food, which, after they circulate through our metabolism, flow through building inlets, outlets and civic infrastructure. Yet, nothing is so far removed from us in modern cities. Water is sourced and energetically pumped from faraway, contested lands before being treated in concealed centralised locations, distanced by their public invisibility. We ventilate our waste gases through mechanical systems while remaining dependent on air regenerated from the most dense forests of our planet, which shrink every year. Food, often grown at the expense of native biodiverse lands, is transported across the globe. As a globally interconnected planet, the essential elements of human survival all suffer from a human-made distribution problem where scarcity in some areas is the result of abundance in others.

Water, air and food are in scarce supply in extreme environments. In fact, all that we have will need to be brought with us, grown and then regenerated. A *Building* rather than a *Planet* will be responsible for the flow and processing of these resources. → p. 144, 164 It is possible to sustain ourselves directly in the spaces where those resources are consumed, at the scale of the habitat, the home, the building, and the city.

Materials
On Earth we often take the availability of steel, concrete, timber, metals and minerals that surround us for granted. All the energy, processing, and transportation that those materials required before they arrived in their "final forms" is easily forgotten. The "embodied energy" of materials has become a critical discussion point for policy makers, especially in relation to their carbon emissions. In turn, the use of non-renewable resources and intensive manufacturing processes is becoming less and less favourable. Similarly, in space we cannot continue to load a launch rocket full of high mass building materials whenever we wish to construct something new. When we descend to the surface of distant planets more frequently we discover similar chemical compositions and materials capable of being roads, bricks, walls, roofs, and furnishings. Ingenuity in local ("in-situ") → p. 106 and low energy material processes move us closer to "living with the land", wherever in the universe that land may be.

Lunar Architecture will look different because it is defined by local materials available on the planetary surface and it will be made differently because of the basic tools we have to work with once there. Like longlasting, low-carbon, vernacular Earth architecture, reliant only on dirt and sunlight, Lunar architecture will combine these well-practised techniques with innovative technologies to sustain future populations on the Moon. → p. 90

Energy
Over half of the energy used in the building sector lights, heats, cools, and ventilates buildings. Dense, high, urban environments create even more need for light, cooling, and ventilation. Passive design, which reduces the need for additional heating or cooling by working with the local climate, is not a new practice. In fact it is older than new — it is ancient — and derived from the relationship between the climate and the body. Perhaps a building's most essential function is in the creation of a boundary that changes the environment "inside" from the one

"outside". Perhaps nothing is more extreme than this boundary in outer space where the pressure difference between life and vacuum could not be clearer.

Turning to the energy of metabolism in their work, LIQUIFER reminds us to capitalise on the synergistic functional systems that we need to live, by combining systems which remediate air and water and produce food, with those that are a source of energy. → p. 164 These methods of working with the interior environment give a new perspective on working seamlessly with nature rather than subduing it by the brute force of machinery.

Given the intensity of these *Architectural* problems on Earth and their relationship to design for outer space, one might ask why even involve the aerospace engineers in questions of habitation for space? This is an issue clearly within the domain of the built environment experts. Traditionally pedagogical and cultural differences between architecture, engineering, and the sciences have kept these problem spaces and their innovations separate. These silos have done little for such complex and interconnected problems. Rather, the common motivations of each discipline provide guiding principles that demonstrate the potential for the co-development of systems essential to sustainable practice and innovation. Such principles can be applied to building on Earth and in space. The intellectual problem space of *Architecture* is systems-based, and we will need integrated efforts across disciplines to inform truly sustainable practice.

Perhaps in this synthetic and interdisciplinary effort, architects, engineers, and scientists will come back to working with the essential tools of life – energy and materials – with a renewed perspective. And, perhaps, this will allow us to welcome a new relationship with our planet. A relationship that reinforces our stewardship of it, our curiosity about it, and our wonder for the miracle of our existence. Armed with renewed love for our home and origins, brandished with a new perspective on the relationship between our bodies and our environment, and with lessons learned from the failures of planetary exploitation, we can more confidently take the first steps to explore alien worlds. Until the next steps in our evolution, we will go out into space not as human beings alone but from spacesuit to spaceship to space city: as a total interconnected and interdependent environment, a total *Architecture*.

LIQUIFER   Page   Project

                                           FFG Office
                                           Office Conversion Vienna

                                           EXOMARS Rover
                                           Aurora program flagship mission

                                           FIPES
                                           Facility for Integrated Planetary
                                           Exploration Simulation

                                           SKYLAB 5
                                           Exhibition at ZOOM Children's Museum Vienna

                                           VisitAir
                                           Information Center, Vienna International Airport

                                           Befleckte Erkenntnis
                                           Installation at Planetarium, Vienna

                                           All Live Differently
                                           Living in the Future housing competition

                                           MOKI
                                           Mobile Childrens Museum Competition

                                           Deployable Getaway
                                           Transformable office furniture

                                   124   Deployable Getaway ISS
                                           Foldable relaxation space for the
                                           International Space Station

                                   98   RAMA
                                           Mobile Research Laboratory

                                           BIOS
                                           Permanent Exhibition at BIOS National Park Center,
                                           Carinthia, Austria

                                           Home on the Moon
                                           Private residence renovation Vienna

                                   126   ISS-Sleep Kit
                                           A sleeping bag for zero gravity

                                           BIORNAMETICS
                                           Biomimetic Proto-Architecture

                                   74   FASTER Forward Acquisition of Soil and Terrain
                                           for Exploration Rover
                                           Cooperative Rovers Development for Moon and Mars

                                   194   Medusa
                                           Future inflatable space habitats for
                                           underwater space simulation

                                   52   SHEE
                                           Planetary Habitat Testbed

                                   156   GrAB
                                           Architectural concepts for growing structures

                                           Space Exhibiton
                                           Exhibition design and implementation at the
                                           Vienna Museum of Science and Technology

Timeline of work

2004

2004

2005–2006

Sep 2005–Mar 2006

2006–2007

Jun–Jul 2006

2007

2007

2007

2007–2009

Nov 2007–Feb 2009

March 2008–April 2009

2010

2010–2012

2010–2013

Nov 2011–Nov 2014

2012

Jan 2013–Dec 2015

May 2013–Feb 2016

Oct 2013–Jan 2015

Page	Project
64, 188	**Moonwalk** — Human-Robot Collaboration for Exploration
	Erdöl & Erdgas — Exhibiton design and implementation at the Vienna Museum of Science and Technology
	LUNA — Artificial Lunar analogues
70	**LavaHive** — 3D printed Mars Habitat
	Moondive — Future mission scenario design for underwater simulation and testing
146	**Eden-ISS** — Greenhouse for extreme environments
90	**RegoLight** — Sintering regolith with solar light for Lunar habitats
166	**Living Architecture** — Selectively programmable bioreactor for buildings
	URBAN — Building a 3D printed Lunar base using circular recycling systems
118	**Gateway I-Hab** — International Habitation Module for the Lunar Orbital Platform
	SynBio4Flav — Novel ways to harvest flavanoids with synthetic microbial consortia
	Co-Corporeality — Responsive, living material systems
	TRAILER — Robotic rover cooperation architectures
102	**Smartie** — Smart resource management based on IoT
	Paving the Road — Large area sintering of regolith
	A-Loop — Post-ISS Commercial Space Station
	Harmonise — Hardware recycling for Lunar and Martian settlement
	This is (not) Rocket Science! — Space science informed by citizen scientists
	LUWEX — Lunar water extraction and purification

Timeline of work

Nov 2013–Oct 2016

May 2014–Oct 2014

Sep 2014–Oct 2015

Jan–Aug 2015

Mar 2015–Aug 2018

Mar 2015–Feb 2019

Nov 2015–Apr 2018

Apr 2016–Jun 2019

Jan 2018–Nov 2018

Jul 2018–Sep 2019 / June 2020 – ongoing

Jan 2019–Aug 2023

May 2019–Apr 2022

Jul 2019–Aug 2021

Mar–Nov 2021

Jun 2021–Dec 2022

Dec 2021–Jun 2023

Sep 2022–Sep 2024

Sep 2022–Sep 2025

Nov 2022–Oct 2024

Acronyms

General

AIAA	American Institute of Aeronautics and Astronautics
A(L)M	Additive (Layer) Manufacturing
CSA	Chinese Space Agency
ECLSS	Environmental Control Life Support System/s
ESA	European Space Agency
EVA	Extravehicular Activity/s
HVAC	Heating, Ventilation, and Air Conditioning
ISS	International Space Station
ISRU	In Situ Resource Utilisation
IVA	Intravehicular Activity/s
LEO	Low Earth orbit
LSS	Life Support System/s
MTF	Mobile Test Facility
NASA	National Aeronautics and Space Administration
NewSpace	Commercial, entrepreneurial, and private space launch and exploration companies and activities
PLSS	Portable Life Support System
SETI	Search for Extraterrestrial Intelligence
TAS-I	Thales Alenia Space Italy
TRL	Technology Readiness Level

Project

FASTER	The Forward Acquisition of Soil and Terrain for Exploration Rover
GrAB	Growing As Building
LIAR	Living Architecture
SHEE	Self-deployable Habitat for Extreme Environments
Smartie	Smart Resource Management based on Internet of Things to support off-Earth manufacturing of Lunar infrastructures
RAMA	Rover for Advanced Mission Applications

References

Travelling through the Extraterrestrial
p. 22–36

1. Díaz, E. (2018) We are all Aliens. *E-Flux.* 81. Available at: https://www.e-flux.com/journal/91/197883/we-are-all-aliens/ [Last accessed: 20 Jul 2022].

2. Mazé, R. (2017) 'Design and the Future: Temporal Politics of 'Making a Difference". In: *Design Anthropological Futures.* R. C. Smith, K. T. Vangkilde, M. G. Kjaersgaard et al. (Eds.) London & New York: Routledge.

3. Loeb, A. (2021) *Extraterrestrial: The First Sign of Intelligent Life Beyond Earth.* Boston, MA: Mariner Books.

4. SETI is an acronym for 'Search for Extraterrestrial Intelligence'.

5. Tarter, J. & Tippett, K. (2020) Jill Tarter: It takes a Cosmos to make a Human. *On Being with Krista Tippett.* First Broadcast: 27 Feb 2020. Available at: https://onbeing.org/programs/jill-tarter-it-takes-a-cosmos-to-make-a-human/ [Last Accessed 20 Jul 2022].

6. Emmett, A. (2017) Hibernation for Space Voyages. *Air Space Magazine.* Available at: https://www.airspacemag.com/space/hibernation-for-space-voyages-180962394/ [Last accessed: 22 Jul 2022].

7. Tsiolkovsky, K. E. (1911) Letter written by K. E. Tsiolkovskiy to B. N. Vorob'yev, 19 Aug 1911.

8. Clarke, A. C. (1997) *3001: The Final Odyssey.* New York: Ballantine Books.

9. Morgan, R. (2002) *Altered Carbon.* London: The Ballantine Book Publishing Group.

10. Fuller, R. B. (1969). *Operating manual for spaceship earth.* New York: Simon and Schuster.

11. Kubrick, S., & Clarke, A. C. (1968). *2001: A space odyssey.* United States: Metro-Goldwyn-Mayer Corp.

12. Treaty on Principles Governing the Activities of States in the Exploration and Use of Outer Space, including the Moon and Other Celestial Bodies (Outer Space Treaty), opened for signature Jan. 27, 1967 18 UST 2410; 610 UNTS 205; 6 ILM 386 (1967).

13. Bauer, C. Bausmeyer, J., Claros, P. M. et al. (2019) Sustainable Moon. *ISU Team Project Report.* Illkirch-Graffenstaden (France) : International Space University.

14. Treaty on Principles Governing the Activities of States in the Exploration and Use of Outer Space, including the Moon and Other Celestial Bodies (Outer Space Treaty), opened for signature Jan. 27, 1967 18 UST 2410; 610 UNTS 205; 6 ILM 386 (1967).

15. The Artemis Accords: Principles for Cooperation in the Civil Exploration and Use of the Moon, Mars, Comets, and Asteroids (2020), https://www.nasa.gov/specials/artemis-accords/img/Artemis-Accords-signed-13Oct2020.pdf [https:// perma.cc/9RM7-EFAE].[Last accessed 26 Jan 2023].

16. The Antarctic Treaty, 402 U.N.T.S. 71, entered into force June 23, 1961. Protocol on Environmental Protection to the Environmental Treaty entered into force 1991

17. The Millenium Charter was authored collectively at a Space Architecture workshop organised by the AIAA DETC Aerospace Architecture Subcommittee in October 2002 at the World Space Congress in Houston.

18. (2002) *The Millenium Charter. Fundamental Principles of Space Architecture.* AIAA DETC Aerospace Architecture Subcommittee Space Architecture Workshop. Houston, Texas, USA: 12 October 2002. Available at: https://spacearchitect.org/wp-content/uploads/2020/06/The-Millennium-Charter.pdf [Last Accessed: 20 Jul 2022].

19. Bannova, O., Clar, R. & Sherwood B. (2008) "The Architecture of Space: Tools for Development In the 21st Century." in *Proc. of the International Astronautical Conference.* Glasgow, Scotland, 29 Sept – 3 Oct 2008.

Designing for Outer Space: An Extreme Environment
p. 40–43

1. Armstrong, R. (2016) *Star Ark: A Living, Self-Sustaining Spaceship.* Springer: New York, NY: 300.

2. Space Architecture Technical Committee (2020) SATC Charter. *Space Architect.* Available from: http://spacearchitect.org/wp-content/uploads/2020/06/SATC-Charter.pdf. [Last accessed 6 Jun 2023].

3. These collaborations are not limited to individuals from these disciplines, however are often dominated by them.

4. Cohen, M. (2022). Innovation and Tradition in Human Spaceflight Architecture. Keynote Address, University of Lisbon Faculty of Architecture.

5. Ciardullo, C. Pailes-Friedman, R., Morris, M. et al. (2022) Bringing it Home: Finding Synergies Between Earth and Space Construction and Design. *51st International Conference on Environmental Systems ICES-2022-336 Proceedings.* St. Paul, Minnesota, 10–14 July 2022.

6. Häuplik-Meusburger, S. Bishop, S. L & Wise, J. A. (2022) Habitability and the Golden Rule of Space Architecture. *51st International Conference on Environmental Systems ICES-2022-336 Proceedings.* St. Paul, Minnesota, 10–14 July 2022.

7. Finckenor, M. M. (2018) Aerospace Materials and Applications. NASA. Available from: https://ntrs.nasa.gov/citations/20160013391 [Last Accessed: 20 Jul 2022].

8. Ciardullo, C. Pailes-Friedman, R., Morris, M. et al. (2022) Bringing it Home: Finding Synergies Between Earth and Space Construction and Design. *51st International Conference on Environmental Systems ICES-2022-336 Proceedings.* St. Paul, Minnesota, 10–14 July 2022.

9. Buchli, V. (2013) *An Anthropology of Architecture.* Routledge: London & New York.

References

The Pursuit of Adaptability
p. 80–81

1. Häuplik-Meusburger, S. Bishop, S. L & Wise, J. A. (2022) Habitability and the Golden Rule of Space Architecture. *51st International Conference on Environmental Systems ICES- 2022-336 Proceedings.* St. Paul, Minnesota, 10–14 July 2022.

The New Vernacular in Outer Space
p. 106–107

1. Jones, H. W. (2018) 'The Recent Large Reduction in Space Launch Cost.' *48th International Conference on Environmental Systems Proceedings.* Albuquerque, New Mexico, 8–12 July 2018.
2. Benaroya, H, Cannon, K. & Imhof, B. (2022) *Habitats on Moon and Mars built from local material.* Space Specials with Barbara Imhof and guests Haym Benaroya & Kevin Cannon. Radio Orange. First Broadcast: 17.05.2022, Available at: https://cba.fro.at/557370. [Last Accessed 6 Jul 2023].
3. Moses, R. W. & Bushnell, D. M. (2016) *Frontier In-Situ Resource Utilization for Enabling Sustained Human Presence on Mars.* USA: NASA. Available at: https://ntrs.nasa.gov/citations/20160005963. [Last Accessed: 22 Jul 2022].
4. Benaroya, H, Cannon, K. & Imhof, B. (2022) *Habitats on Moon and Mars built from local material.* Space Specials with Barbara Imhof and guests Haym Benaroya & Kevin Cannon. Radio Orange. First Broadcast: 17.05.2022, Available at: https://cba.fro.at/557370. [Last Accessed: 22 Jul 2022].

When the Natural State is Motion
p. 131–132

1. Meggs, L. (2017) From Tools to Trash: Marshall's Payload Stowage Team Tracks It. *NASA.* Available from: https://www.nasa.gov/mission_pages/station/research/payload_stowage [Last Accessed: 17 Jan 2023].
2. NASA. (2012, Nov 19) Departing Space Station Commander Provides Tour of Orbital Laboratory. [Video file.]. *YouTube.* https://www.youtube.com/watch?v=d0N4t5NKW-k. [Last Accessed: 17 Jan 2023].
3. Atkinson, N. (2021) Since There's no Up or Down in Space, How do our Brains Deal With This? *Universe Today.* Available from: https://www.universetoday.com/149559/since-theres-no-up-or-down-in-space-how-do-our-brains-deal-with-this/ [Last Accessed: 17 Jan 2023].

Replicating Terrestrial Systems
p. 135–137

1. The timeframe at which moderate concentration levels of toxins or pathogens reveal their impacts may only become clear over long periods of time.
2. ESA (2019) New life support system cleans air during full-house Space Station. *ESA.* Available at: https://www.esa.int/Science_Exploration/Human_and_Robotic_Exploration/New_life_support_system_cleans_air_during_full-house_Space_Station [Last Accessed: 26 Jan 2023].
3. Generic, R. J. (2008) Mission Operations Directorate. *Operations Division: National Aeronautics and Space Administration: Lyndon B. Johnson Space Center Houston, Texas.* Available at: https://nasa.gov/centers/johnson/pdf/359891main_125_MAL_G_J_2_E1.pdf [Last Accessed: 5 Sep 2022].
4. NASA (2019) Spacewalk Spacesuit Basics. *NASA.* Available at: https://www.nasa.gov/feature/spacewalk-spacesuit-basics [Last Accessed: 26 July 2022].
5. Renamed the Life Support Systems Integration Facility (LSSIF), see citation below.
6. Connolly, J. H. (2002) 'Architecture'. In: Lane, H. W., Sauer, R. L., Feeback, D. L., eds. *Isolation: NASA Experiments in Closed-Environment Living: Advanced Human Life Support Enclosed System Final Report.* San Diego: Univelt, Incorporated. pp. 131-139.
7. *Ibid.*

Mission Preparation: Simulating Future Explorations
p. 175–177

1. Zhang, J. (2021) LUNAR PALACE 1 based space food and nutrition research. In Proceedings: 43rd COSPAR Scientific Assembly. 28 January – 4 February.; Space.com Staff (2018) Lunar Palace 1: China's One-Year Mock Moon Mission in Pictures. *Space.* Available at: https://www.space.com/40610-china-mock-moon-mission-Lunar-palace-1-photos.html [Last accessed: 26 Jan 2023].
2. Mingzhu, L. (2020) Lunar Palace 1: To the Moon and Beyond. *Beihang University.* Available at: https://ev.buaa.edu.cn/info/1103/2695.htm [Last accessed: 26 Jan 2023].
3. Hao, Z., Zhu, Y., Feng, S. & Meng, C. (2019) Effects of long term isolation on the emotion change of "Lunar Palace 365" crewmembers. *Science Bulletin.* 64(13). DOI:10.1016/j.scib.2019.05.019.
4. Popper, J. & Imhof, B. (2018) The Joy of Sets presents Capricorn Two: A Mars Mission Simulation. *69th International Astronautical Congress (IAC) Proceedings,* Bremen, Germany, 1-5 October 2018.
5. Amils, R., Fernández-Remolar, D., & The Ipbsl Team (2014). Río tinto: a geochemical and mineralogical terrestrial analogue of Mars. *Life (Basel, Switzerland), 4*(3), 511–534. https://doi.org/10.3390/life4030511.
6. Imhof, B., Hogle, M., Davenport, B. et al. (2017) Project Moonwalk: lessons learnt from testing human robot collaboration scenarios in a Lunar and Martian simulation. *68th International Astronautical Congress (IAC) Proceedings,* Adelaide, Australia, 25–29 September 2017.
7. Allouis, E., Marc, R. Gancet, J. et al. (2017) FP7 FASTER project – Demonstration of Multiplatform Operation for Safer Planetary Traverses. 14th Symposium on Advanced Space Technologies in Robotics and Automation Proceedings, Leiden, The Netherlands, 20–22 June 2017.
8. Executive Study: Moonwalk, Moonwalk Consortium (2016) Executive Study: Moonwalk. Available at: https://liquifer.com/moonwalk-executive-summary-october-2016/ [Last Accessed: 19 Jun 2023].

References

The Space–Earth Continuum
p. 204–207

1. Sagan, C. (1994) Pale Blue Dot:Pale Blue Dot: A Vision of the Human Future in Space. New York: Random House.

2. Lovelock, J. (1979) *Gaia: A New Look at Life on Earth.* Oxford: Oxford University Press.

3. Klepeis, N. E., et al. (2001) The National Human Activity Pattern Survey (NHAPS): A Resource for Assessing Exposure to Environmental Pollutants. *Journal of Exposure Science & Environmental Epidemiology.* 11(3): 231–52, https://doi.org/10.1038/sj.jea.7500165.

4. United Nations Environment Programme. (2022) *2022 Global Status Report for Buildings and Construction: Towards Zero-emission, Efficient and Resilient Buildings and Construction Sector.* United Nations Environment Program. Available at: https://globalabc.org/sites/default/files/2022-11/FULL%20REPORT_2022%20Buildings-GSR_1.pdf. [Last Accessed: 4 Apr 2023].

5. Ciardullo, C. Pailes-Friedman, R., Morris, M. et al. (2022) Bringing it Home: Finding Synergies Between Earth and Space Construction and Design. 51st International Conference on Environmental Systems ICES-2022-336. 10-14.07.2022, St. Paul, Minnesota.

CAVEAT
Sources:

– The quotes that appear throughout this volume have been taken from Barbara Imhof's Space Specials, a podcast series that she has hosted since 2006. This is also true for the excerpts included in the Antarctic and Pacific Island Expeditions. All of these episodes are stored on the Cultural Broadcasting Archive website, which can be accessed here: https://cba.fro.at/podcast/space-specials.

Planetary Specification References

Mars
p. 47

1. NASA Content Administrator (2008) Valles Marineris: The Grand Canyon of Mars. *NASA.* Available at: https://www.nasa.gov/multimedia/imagegallery/image_feature_83.html. [Last Accessed: 27 Feb 2023].

2. De La Torre L. B. (2022) What is the Habitable Zone? *NASA Exoplanet Exploration: Planets Beyond our Solar System.* Available at: https://exoplanets.nasa.gov/resources/2255/what-is-the-habitable-zone/. [Last Accessed: 27 Feb 2023].

3. Wall, M. (2021) Mars was always too small to hold onto its oceans, rivers and lakes. *Space.* Available at: https://www.space.com/mars-too-small-ocean-rivers-lakes. [Last Accessed: 27 Feb 2023].

4. Cooper, K. (2022) Massive Mars dust storms triggered by heat imbalances, scientists find. *Space.* Available at: https://www.space.com/mars-climate-dust-storms-heat-imbalance. [Last Accessed: 27 Feb 2023].

5. *Ibid.*

6. Wernicke, L. J., & Jakosky, B. M. (2021). Martian hydrated minerals: A significant water sink. *Journal of Geophysical Research*: Planets, 126.

7. Wernicke, L. J., & Jakosky, B. M. (2021). Martian hydrated minerals: A significant water sink. *Journal of Geophysical Research*: Planets, 126., NASA Content Administrator (2008) Valles Marineris: The Grand Canyon of Mars. *NASA.* Available at: https://www.nasa.gov/multimedia/imagegallery/image_feature_83.html. [Last Accessed: 27 Feb 2023].

8. Maderer, J. (2021) Making Martian Rocket BioFuel on Mars. *Georgia Tech College of Engineering.* Available at: https://coe.gatech.edu/news/2021/10/making-martian-rocket-biofuel-mars. [Last Accessed: 27 Feb 2023]., Kruyer, N. S. Realff, M. J., Sun, W. et al. (2021) Designing the bioproduction of Martian rocket propellant via a biotechnology-enabled in situ resource utilization strategy. *Nature Communications.* 12:6166. https://doi.org/10.1038/s41467-021-26393-7.

9. David. L. (2013) Toxic Mars: Astronauts Must Deal with Perchlorate on the Red Planet. *Space.* Available at: https://www.space.com/21554-mars-toxic-perchlorate-chemicals.html. [Last Accessed: 27 Feb 2023].

10. Economou, T. et. al. (1997) The Chemical Composition of Martian Rocks and Soil: Preliminary Analyses. Available at: https://mars.nasa.gov/MPF/science/lpsc98/1711.pdf. [Last Accessed: 27 Feb 2023].

11. Schleppi, J. Gibbons, J. Groetsch, A. et al. (2018) Manufacture of glass and mirrors from Lunar regolith simulant. *Journal of Material Science.* 54:3726–3747. https://doi.org/10.1007/s10853-018-3101-y.

Mars Table Sources:

– Williams, D. (2021) Planetary Factsheet Mars. *NASA Solar System Exploration.* Available at: https://nssdc.gsfc.nasa.gov/planetary/factsheet/marsfact.html. [Last Accessed: 27 Feb 2023].

– Barnett, A. (2022) Mars by the Numbers. *NASA Solar System Exploration..* Available at: https://solarsystem.nasa.gov/planets/mars/by-the-numbers/. [Last Accessed: 27 Feb 2023].

– Davis. P. (2021) Mars In Depth. *NASA Solar System Exploration.* Available at: https://solarsystem.nasa.gov/planets/mars/in-depth/. [Last Accessed: 27 Feb 2023].

– Turner, J., Anderson, P., Lachlan-Cope, T. et al. (2009). Record low surface air temperature at Vostok station, Antarctica. *Journal of Geophysical Research.* 114:D24. doi:10.1029/2009JD012104

– El Fadli, K. I., Cerveny, R. S. Burt. C. C. et al. (2013) World Meteorological Organization Assessment of the Purported World Record 58°C Temperature Extreme at El Azizia, Libya (13 September 1922). *Bulletin of the American Meteorological Society.* 94:2. https://doi.org/10.1175/BAMS-D-12-00093.1.

Planetary Specification References

The Moon
p. 85

1. Plain, C. (2020) NASA finds evidence two early planets collided to form Moon. *NASA*. Available at: https://www.nasa.gov/feature/nasa-finds-evidence-two-early-planets-collided-to-form-moon [Last Accessed: 27 Feb 2023].

2. Mathewson, S. (2018) Days on Earth Are Getting Longer, Thanks to the Moon. *Space*. Available at: https://www.space.com/40802-earth-days-longer-moon-movement.html. [Last Accessed: 27 Feb 2023].

3. Davis, P. (2022) Earth's Moon Overview. *NASA Solar System Exploration*. Available at: https://solarsystem.nasa.gov/moons/earths-moon/overview/. [Last Accessed: 27 Feb 2023].

4. Mathewson, S. (2017) 'Levitating' Moon Dust Explained in New NASA Study. *Space*. Available at: https://www.space.com/35240-moon-dust-levitates-nasa-study.html. [Last accessed: 27 Feb 2023].

5. Harbaugh, J. (2022) Fission Surface Power, Technology Demonstration Missions. *NASA*. Available at: https://www.nasa.gov/mission_pages/tdm/fission-surface-power/index.html [Last Accessed: 27 Feb 2023].

6. ESA (2019) Helium-3 mining on the Lunar surface. *ESA*. Available at: https://www.esa.int/Enabling_Support/Preparing_for_the_Future/Space_for_Earth/Energy/Helium-3_mining_on_the_Lunar_surface [Last Accessed: 27 Feb 2023].

7. Strickland, A. (2022) Plants have been grown in Lunar soil for the 1st time ever. *CNN*. Available at: https://edition.cnn.com/2022/05/12/world/plants-Lunar-soil-scn/index.html [Last Accessed: 27 Feb 2023].

Moon Table Sources:

– Williams, D. (2021) Planetary Factsheet Moon. *NASA*. Available at: https://nssdc.gsfc.nasa.gov/planetary/factsheet/moonfact.html. [Last Accessed: 27 Feb 2023].

– Barnett, A. (2022) Earth's Moon by the Numbers. *NASA*. Available at: https://solarsystem.nasa.gov/moons/earths-moon/by-the-numbers/. [Last Accessed: 27 Feb 2023].

– Hille, K. (2020) LUNAR RECONNAISSANCE ORBITER: Temperature Variation on the Moon. *NASA*. Available at: https://Lunar.gsfc.nasa.gov/images/lithos/LROlitho7temperaturevariation27May2014.pdf. [Last Accessed: 27 Feb 2023].

– Davis, P. (2022) Earth's Moon In Depth. *NASA Solar System Exploration*. Available at: https://solarsystem.nasa.gov/moons/earths-moon/in-depth/. [Last Accessed: 27 Feb 2023].

– Turner, J., Anderson, P., Lachlan-Cope, T. et al. (2009). Record low surface air temperature at Vostok station, Antarctica. *Journal of Geophysical Research*. 114:D24. https://doi.org/10.1029/2009JD012104.

– El Fadli, K. I., Cerveny, R. S. Burt. C. C. et al. (2013) World Meteorological Organization Assessment of the Purported World Record 58°C Temperature Extreme at El Azizia, Libya (13 September 1922). *Bulletin of the American Meteorological Society*. 94:2. https://doi.org/10.1175/BAMS-D-12-00093.1.

Orbit
p. 113

1. J. (2022) Recycling in space: Wannabe or Reality? *European Space Agency*. Available at: https://blogs.esa.int/cleanspace/2022/01/10/recycling-in-space-wannabe-or-reality/. [Last Accessed: 27 Feb 2023].

Orbital Table Sources:

– Mars, K. (2022) Gateway. *NASA*. Available at: https://www.nasa.gov/gateway. [Last Accessed: 27 Feb 2023].

– ESA (2018) Reaching the Space Station Infographic. *ESA*. Available at: https://www.esa.int/ESA_Multimedia/Images/2018/06/Reaching_the_Space_Station_infographic. [Last Accessed: 27 Feb 2023].

– Gerstenmaier, W. & Crusan, J. (2018) CisLunar and Gateway Overview. *NASA*. Available at: https://www.nasa.gov/sites/default/files/atoms/files/cisLunar-update-gerstenmaier-crusan-v5a_tagged_0.pdf. [Last Accessed: 27 Feb 2023].

– Frost, R. (2017) What are the highest and lowest points in the orbit of the ISS? *Forbes*. Available at: https://www.forbes.com/sites/quora/2017/03/15/what-are-the-highest-and-lowest-points-in-the-orbit-of-the-iss/?sh=583709a74053. [Last Accessed: 27 Feb 2023].

– NASA (2020) Astronauts answer student questions. *NASA Johnson*. Available at: https://www.nasa.gov/centers/johnson/pdf/569954main_astronaut%20_FAQ.pdf. [Last Accessed: 27 Feb 2023].

– Adamek, C. (2019) Gateway System Requirements. *NASA*. Available at: https://ntrs.nasa.gov/api/citations/20190029153/downloads/20190029153.pdf. [Last Accessed: 27 Feb 2023].

– ESA with Oldenburg, K. (2021) Temperatures on the Space Station. Available at: https://www.esa.int/ESA_Multimedia/Images/2021/08/Temperatures_on_the_Space_Station. [Last Accessed: 27 Feb 2023].

– Hille, K. (2014) Lunar Reconnaissance Orbiter. *NASA*. Available at: https://Lunar.gsfc.nasa.gov/images/lithos/LROlitho7temperaturevariation27May2014.pdf. [Last Accessed: 27 Feb 2023].

– Brown, M. (2022) NASA Lunar Gateway: Launch Window, Specs and Orbit of the Moon's Space Station. *Inverse*. Available at: https://www.inverse.com/innovation/nasa-Lunar-gateway-codex. [Last Accessed: 27 Feb 2023].

Planetary Specification References

Earth
p. 141

1. Richie, H. (2019) Half of the world's habitable land is used for agriculture. *Our World in Data*. Available at: https://ourworldindata.org/global-land-for-agriculture. [Last Accessed: 1 Mar 2023].

2. Hayes, J.M. (2016) Evolution of the Atmosphere. *Britannica*. Available at: https://www.britannica.com/topic/evolution-of-the-atmosphere-1703862 [Last accessed 10 Jan 2023].

3. Buis, A. (2019) Earth's Atmosphere: A Multi-layered Cake. NASA *Global Climate Change*. Available at: https://climate.nasa.gov/news/2919/earths-atmosphere-a-multi-layered-cake/ [Last accessed 10 Jan 2023].

Earth Table Sources:

- Williams, D. (2021) Earth Factsheet. *NASA*. Available at: https://nssdc.gsfc.nasa.gov/planetary/factsheet/earthfact.html. [Last accessed 10 Jan 2023].

- Barnett, A. (2022) Earth By the Numbers. *NASA*. Available at: https://solarsystem.nasa.gov/planets/earth/by-the-numbers/. [Last accessed 10 Jan 2023].

- Turner, J., Anderson, P., Lachlan-Cope, T. et al. (2009). Record low surface air temperature at Vostok station, Antarctica. *Journal of Geophysical Research*. 114:D24. https://doi.org/10.1029/2009JD012104

- El Fadli, K. I., Cerveny, R. S. Burt. C. C. et al. (2013) World Meteorological Organization Assessment of the Purported World Record 58°C Temperature Extreme at El Azizia, Libya (13 September 1922). *Bulletin of the American Meteorological Society*. 94:2. https://doi.org/10.1175/BAMS-D-12-00093.1.

Underwater
p. 183

1. National Ocean Service (2002) Sound waves propagate faster than in air. *National Oceanic and Atmospheric Administration*. Available at: https://oceanexplorer.noaa.gov/explorations/sound01/background/acoustics/acoustics.html [Last Accessed: 4 Apr 2023].

2. Mondal, A. & Banerjee, S. (2022) Effect of productivity and seasonal variation on phytoplankton intermittency in a microscale ecological study using closure approach. Sci Rep 12:5939. https://doi.org/10.1038/s41598-022-09420-5.

3. National Ocean Service (2010) Where is all of Earth's water? *National Oceanic and Atmospheric Administration*. Available at: https://oceanservice.noaa.gov/facts/wherewater.html. [Last Accessed: 4 Apr 2023].

4. National Ocean Service (2010) Thermohaline Circulation. *National Oceanic and Atmospheric Administration*. Available at: https://oceanservice.noaa.gov/education/tutorial_currents/05conveyor1.html. [Last Accessed: 4 Apr 2023].

5. ESA (2019) Learning to live with the laws of motion. ESA. Available at: https://www.esa.int/Science_Exploration/Human_and_Robotic_Exploration/Astronauts/Learning_to_live_with_the_laws_of_motion. [Last Accessed: 4 Apr 2023].

Underwater Table Sources:

- USGS (2022) Why is the Ocean Salty? *U.S. Department of the Interior*. Available at: https://www.usgs.gov/faqs/why-ocean-salty. [Last accessed 10 Jan 2023].

- Allaby (1994) Euphotic Zone. *European Environmental Agency*. Available at: https://www.eea.europa.eu/help/glossary/eea-glossary/euphotic-zone. [Last accessed 10 Jan 2023].

- National Ocean Service (2021) How does pressure change with ocean depth? *National Oceanic and Atmospheric Administration*. Available at: https://oceanservice.noaa.gov/facts/pressure.html. [Last accessed 10 Jan 2023].

- Wikipedia (2022) Underwater Acoustics. *Wikipedia*. Available at: https://en.wikipedia.org/wiki/Underwater_acoustics. [Last accessed 10 Jan 2023].

- Levy, R. (2022) Sea Surface Temperature. NASA *Earth Observatory*. Available at: https://earthobservatory.nasa.gov/global-maps/MYD28M. [Last accessed 10 Jan 2023].

Biographies

LIQUIFER
is a microenterprise with a base in Vienna, Austria, and another in Bremen, Germany. LIQUIFER is committed to collaborative work with international partners from a wide array of disciplines. A small core team with the support of associated experts make it possible that LIQUIFER plays a valuable role in the field of human space exploration.

LIQUIFER Core Team

Barbara Imhof trained as an architect under Wolf D. Prix of Coop Himmelb(l)au. She holds a PhD from the University of Technology Vienna and a Masters in Space Studies from the International Space University. She is a Space Architect, design researcher, and educator. Following her Masters at ISU Barbara interned at NASA Johnson Space Centre, supporting the design of a large simulator for a human mission to Mars as part of Project BIOPLEX. Her work focuses on designing for extreme environments and space. With these she combines two main work paths: one follows designing systems, mission elements and habitats for living beyond the Earth's atmosphere and the other path translates biological role models into the design of architecture. She enjoys working across disciplines and in the past 20 years has collaborated with a wide selection of well-known artists, most notably during her time on the research vessel for the 1st Antarctic Biennale in 2017 and then in 2018 as part of the SUPERFLEX Deep Sea Minding project run by TBA21 Academy. She has an extensive record of teaching (space) design and architecture at universities worldwide most recently as Adjunct Faculty at ISU and as a Project Lead on a number of FWF funded projects at "die Angewandte". Additionally, Barbara has been producing the Space Specials podcast for more than 10 years.

Waltraut Hoheneder holds a diploma in architecture from the Academy of Applied Arts in Vienna, studio Wolf D. Prix and a diploma in commercial sciences from the Vienna University of Economics and Business. She worked in the fields of market research, product and architectural design before becoming a design architect in large-scale projects at Coop Himmelb(l)au until 2003. Together with Barbara Imhof she established LIQUIFER Systems Group as a private company in 2005 after the foundation of LIQUIFER as an association by Barbara Imhof, Susmita Mohanty and Norbert Frischauf in 2003. Waltraut is a senior designer at LIQUIFER Systems Group as well as a co-manager Within this role she focuses on the development of transformable systems and the integration of regenerative infrastructure in building systems. Her recent engagement in research on microbial systems is driven by the huge potential to provide sustainable solutions for contemporary challenges on Earth by implementing these systems into our built environment. Parallel to her work at LIQUIFER she taught within architectural design programmes at the Vienna University of Technology until 2018.

René Waclavicek originally studied architecture at TU Wien. He is a building construction engineer with extensive experience in architecture and design. In addition to his engineering expertise, he was trained as a mason and carpenter. After joining LIQUIFER in 2005, René continued to work on a number of terrestrial construction projects, including the new construction of the Landesberufsschule, Graz with Michael Walraff. His skills are applied in interdisciplinary research as well as in architecture and design, especially in the application of parametric methods and the development of geometries. More recently he has been working with 3D printing technologies to be developed for the Lunar and Martian surface. René was made partner at LIQUIFER in 2019 and has been instrumental in design and visualisation of LIQUIFER's portfolio.

LIQUIFER Co-Founder

Susmita Mohanty trained as an electrical engineer at Gujarat University, Ahmedabad, before completing two Masters degrees, the first in Industrial Design from the National Institute of Design and the second in Space studies from the International Space University in Strasbourg. Her studies finished with a PhD on Integrated High-Fidelity Planetary Mission Simulators from Chalmers University of Technology, Göteborg, Sweden. Susmita is the only space entrepreneur in the world to have co-founded space companies on three different continents: EARTH2ORBIT, Bangalore (2009-2021), LIQUIFER, Vienna (2003-ongoing) and MOONFRONT, San Francisco (2001-07). Prior to becoming an entrepreneur, she worked for the International Space Station Program at Boeing in California and did a short stint at NASA Johnson. In 2021, she launched India's first dedicated space think tank Spaceport SARABHAI. In 2019, Susmita was selected as one of BBC's 100 Women laureates crafting a female-led future. In 2017, she was featured on the cover of Fortune Magazine. She is a member of the World Economic Forum Global Future Council for Space Technologies.

LIQUIFER Consultants

Stephen Ransom gained a BSc honours degree in Aeronautical Engineering at the University of Salford, England. He began his career in the British aerospace industry in 1961. Following work in the UK, Stephen joined ERNO Raumfahrttechnik in Bremen on the Spacelab programme as a systems engineer for the Spacelab Pallet. After a brief return to the aircraft industry with work at Vereinigte Flugtechnische Werke and MBB's Special Projects Division he rejoined the space division of EADS in 1983 in their advanced projects office in Bremen. His work dealt with future spacecraft and planetary exploration including the International Space Station Columbus programme. During this time he undertook studies on robotic missions to the Moon and Mars, space habitats, EURECA utilisation, an unmanned in-orbit recoverable vehicle, and planetary aerobots. He subsequently established himself as an aerospace consultant in 2005 and became an affiliated consultant to LIQUIFER Systems Group. In addition, he has given lectures on space programmes, the history of the development of aerospace technology to the German Aerospace Society and Universities.

Bob Davenport gained a BSc in Physics and an MSc in Materials Science from the University of Leeds. He was a space systems engineer with

40+ years of experience in the development and testing of manned space systems, interface definitions, operations scenarios and payload integration for the European module Columbus on the International Space Station (ISS). Bob began his career with Hawker Siddeley Dynamics in Stevenage, U.K., before joining ERNO Raumfahrttechnik, Bremen, Germany (now Airbus Defence and Space) as systems engineer on the Spacelab project. Concurrently with his Airbus activities, Bob was active as a scientific assistant in the Department of Geosciences, University of Bremen, researching the global carbon cycle using remote sensing. Bob joined LIQUIFER as an internal consultant in 2013 and has since worked on several EU/ESA funded projects such as Moonwalk, TRAILER, URBAN, Eden-ISS, Smartie, I-Hab and Paving The Road.

Chris Gilbert initially trained as an engineer at the University of Leicester and began his professional career as a design engineer at Hawker Siddeley Dynamics (now Airbus Defence and Space) in Stevenage, Hertfordshire, working on launch vehicles and satellites. Following completion of a Master of Business Administration degree at Cranfield School of Business he took up a position as system engineer at ERNO Raumfahrttechnik GmbH (now Airbus Defence and Space) in Bremen, Germany, working on the Spacelab programme. He subsequently developed new responsibilities in marketing, business development and strategy, with particular focus on space exploration and space policy. From 2011 – 2012 he attended the George Washington University's Space Policy Institute in Washington, DC, as a visiting scholar, studying issues of international cooperation in space exploration. Since being associated with LIQUIFER Chris has been involved in a number of projects, providing advice and guidance on management and strategic aspects.

Daniel Schubert studied at the Technical University of Berlin and has an engineering diploma in industrial engineering with an emphasis on aerospace and production techniques. In 2011, he initiated the EDEN group at the DLR Institute of Space Systems for technology investigations on Bio-regenerative Life Support Systems and since served as the team leader of this group. His research expertise is set on habitat interface analysis and plant accommodation and dynamic plant production planning. Throughout many projects for ESA, EU, Bundesministerium für Bildung und Forschung (BMBF), Wirtschaftsförderung Bremen (WfB), Dr. Schubert proved his management- and team leading skills. Outstanding is the Eden – ISS project. He led this project with 15 international partners (incl. LIQUIFER), including the organisation of the deployment mission of the greenhouse system at the Antarctic research station Neumayer III in 2017/18. Daniel's relationship with LIQUIFER started with habitat design studies in 2011 and over the past 10 years has incorporated numerous outreach activities, proposal writing, and engineering expertise.

Monika Lipinska holds a Masters in Architecture from Lund University and a Masters in Space Studies from the International Space University. The focal point of her research during these degrees was on developing architectural and biotechnological solutions for building habitable environments which support human performance and wellbeing in space. During her studies, she worked in architectural offices in Tokyo, Copenhagen, and San Francisco. Currently (2023) she is pursuing her PhD at the Hub for Biotechnology in the Built Environment at Newcastle University in collaboration with NASA Ames Research Centre, where she researches biofabrication strategies for building inhabitable structures on the Moon and Mars. Monika is a co-founder of Bio-Futures for Transplanetary Habitats, a research platform that aims to explore and enable research on transplanetary habitats through an emphasis on biosocial and biotechnological relations. Monika came to LIQUIFER at the beginning of her Space Architecture journey, as a summer intern in 2017. During her continuing studies she gradually began doing research and design work with LIQUIFER before becoming an internal consultant in 2020.

Prologue

Brent Sherwood is a space architect with over 35 years of professional experience in the space industry. He is Senior Vice President, Space Systems Development, for Blue Origin. SSD develops in-space systems for Earth orbital, cislunar, and lunar business. Brent was at the NASA Jet Propulsion Laboratory for 14 years, leading concept and proposal methods and planetary mission formulation. Prior, he was at Boeing for 17 years, leading human exploration concept engineering, space station module manufacturing engineering and commercial space program development. Brent has advanced degrees in architecture (Yale) and aerospace engineering (University of Maryland). He is the 2020 recipient of the American Society of Civil Engineers Columbia Medal and an Associate Fellow of the American Institute of Aeronautics and Astronautics. He edited the book *Out of This World: The New Field of Space Architecture* and has published over 50 papers on the exploration, development and settlement of space.

Epilogue

Christina Ciardullo is an Architect, co-founder of the award-winning space architecture firm SEArch+ and PhD Researcher at the Yale Center for Ecosystems and Architecture. With undergraduate degrees in astronomy and philosophy, and a Masters of Architecture from Columbia University, Christina bridges a career between practice and research at the intersection of the natural sciences and the built environment. She has worked in design positions at New York City Planning, NASA's Habitability Design Center, Ennead Architects, Foster+Partners and LAVA. Supported by a NASA Consortium Grant, she was the 2015/2016 Carnegie Mellon University Anna Kalla Fellow and the 2016 Buckminster Fuller Institute Fellow. In her work with Yale CEA, Christina has collaborated with the United Nations Environment Program on thought leadership in urban agriculture and the embodied and operational carbon of building materials. Committed to work in space that supports sustainable development on Earth, she lectures and publishes on the relationship between energy and resource-efficient practice in space and earth.

Biographies

Editorial Team

Jennifer Cunningham holds a Masters in Material Culture and Design Anthropology from University College London. She works as a researcher, writer and editor within the fields of architecture and design. Her work has been included in Copenhagen Design Biennale, Oslo Architecture Triennale and London Design Festival. Jennifer is pursuing a PhD in Digital Media and Architecture at the University of Lisbon, and is a researching editor with the Future Observatory at the Design Museum in London where she undertakes research and commissions work supporting the UK's response to the climate crisis. Jennifer worked as an associate at LIQUIFER to develop the concept, undertake editorial management and co-author Living Beyond Earth: Architecture for Extreme Environments.

Matthew Ponsford studied Philosophy at University College London. He is a London-based journalist and editor who has written for MIT Technology Review, New Scientist, National Geographic, Thomson Reuters, CNN, The Guardian, Financial Times Weekend, BBC, Deutsche Welle and Wired UK. He is co-leader of The Manuals, a global research project on ecosystem restoration, which has hosted participatory design events at the Tate Modern, The Barbican Centre and Royal Botanic Gardens, Kew. Matt worked on LIQUIFER Living Beyond Earth: Architecture for Extreme Environments as a copy-editor.

Project Support

A number of the projects highlighted in this book would not have been possible without support from the European Union. The following sentences recognise their support, and provide details of the funding.

SHEE: The project has received funding from the European Union's Seventh Framework Programme for research, technological development and demonstration under grant agreement no. 312747.

Moonwalk: The project has received funding from the European Union's Seventh Framework Programme for research, technological development and demonstration under grant agreement no. 607346.

Faster: The project has received funding from the European Union's Seventh Framework Programme for research, technological development and demonstration under grant agreement no. 284419.

RegoLight: This project was funded by Horizon 2020 Research and Innovation Programme, Grant agreement ID: 686202.

Eden ISS: This project was funded by Horizon 2020 Research and Innovation Programme, Grant agreement no. 636501.

Living Architecture: The project has received funding from the European Union's Horizon 2020 Research and Innovation Programme under Grant Agreement no 686585.

Image & Visualisation Credits

Unless otherwise stated below, all photographs are credited to Bruno Stubenrauch and all visualisations are credited to LIQUIFER. Images listed below are copyright to their owner and ordered by page number.

1   Hanno Müller, AWI, 2019
12 Petra Gruber, Robert Fritz, 2004
13 LIQUIFER, 2017
18 Dusty Mars Rover Selfie courtesy of NASA/JPL Caltech, 2012
19 Growing as Building Consortium, photo by Ceren Yönetim, 2013–2015
20 LOLA (Lunar Orbit and Landing Approach), Langley Research Centre Hampton courtesy of NASA, 1963
21 LIQUIFER, 2008
22 see the invisible © Eva Schlegel, Barbara Imhof, Damjan Minovski, Vladimir Romanyuk, 2016
45 Mars Perseverance Sol 2 courtesy of NASA/JPL Caltech, 2021
46 LIQUIFER, 2017
48 Moonwalk Consortium, photo by Comex, 2016
60 Top images: Moonwalk Consortium, photos by Bob Davenport, 2016
60 Bottom image: Moonwalk Consortium, photo by Bruno Stubenrauch, 2016
61–65 Moonwalk Consortium, photos by Bruno Stubenrauch, 2016
66 Top left, bottom: Moonwalk Consortium, photos by Bruno Stubenbacher, 2016
66 Top right: Moonwalk Consortium, photo by Comex, 2016
67 Moonwalk Consortium, photo by Bruno Stubenrauch, 2016
68 Moonwalk Consortium, photo by Bob Davenport, 2016
69 Left: Moonwalk Consortium, photos by LIQUIFER, 2016
69 Top right: Moonwalk Consortium, photo by Comex, 2016
69 Bottom right: Moonwalk Consortium, photo by Bob Davenport, 2016
70 Courtesy of ESA EAC Spaceship, 2015
75–76 FASTER Consortium, 2013
77 Base: FASTER Consortium, photo by LIQUIFER, 2013
83 Moon, Luc Viatour, 2017
84 Buzz Aldrin with Apollo 11 Lunar Module on the Moon courtesy of NASA, 1969
91 Top: RegoLight Consortium, photo by LIQUIFER, 2018
91 Bottom right images courtesy of ESA, 2018
99 Background image courtesy of NASA, visualisation by LIQUIFER, 2009
101 Background image courtesy of NASA, visualisation by LIQUIFER, 2009
103 Smartie Consortium, 2022
111 Canadarm2, ISS, courtesy of NASA, 2020
112 ISS (with docked Soyuz MS-18 to Nauka multipurpose laboratory module) above Typhoon Mindulle courtesy of NASA, 2021
114 Background image courtesy of NASA, visualisation by LIQUIFER, 2019
116, 117, 121 Courtesy of Airbus Defence and Space GmbH, 2019
119 I-HAB visualisation by LIQUIFER and Damjan Minovski
127 Background image courtesy of NASA, visualisation by LIQUIFER, 2012
129 Background image courtesy of NASA, visualisation by LIQUIFER, 2009
139 DLR, 2019
140 LIQUIFER, 2004
142 DLR, 2017
144 DLR, 2018
145 © AWI / Michael Trautmann, 2019
147 Top: Hanno Müller, AWI, 2019
147 Bottom: DLR, 2018
148 Bottom left: DLR, 2017
149 DLR, 2017 & 2018
150 Left: DLR, 2018
152 DLR, 2017
155 Top: Hanno Müller, AWI, 2019
157 Growing as Building Consortium, photos by Damjan Minovski, 2013–2015
159 Top: Growing as Building Consortium, photo by Damjan Minovski, 2013–2015
159 Bottom: Growing as Building Consortium photos by the GrAB team, 2013–2015
160 Top left: Growing as Building Consortium, photo by Angelo Vermeulen, 2013–2015
160 Top right: Growing as Building Consortium, photo by Ceren Yönetim, 2013–2015
160 Bottom: Growing as Building Consortium, photo by the GrAB Team, 2013–2015
161 Growing as Building Consortium, photos by the GrAB Team, 2013–2015
162 Top: Growing as Building Consortium, photos by Angelo Vermeulen, 2013–2015
162 Bottom: Growing as Building Consortium, photos by LIQUIFER, 2013-2015
165 Living Architecture Consortium, visualisation by LIQUIFER and Damjan Minovski, 2019
167 Left: Living Architecture Consortium, photos by LIQUIFER, 2019
170 Bottom right: Living Architecture Consortium, visualisation by LIQUIFER and Damjan Minovski, 2019
171 Living Architecture Consortium, photo by LIQUIFER, 2019
173 Living Architecture Consortium, visualisation by LIQUIFER and Damjan Minovski, 2019
181 LIQUIFER, 2017
182 LIQUIFER, 2008
184 Moonwalk Consortium, photo by Comex, 2016
186–193 Moonwalk Consortium, photo by Comex 2016
196–198 LIQUIFER, 2017
200, 202, 203 LIQUIFER, 2018
224 Curiosity Conducting Mini-Drill Test at 'Mojave' courtesy of NASA, 2015

Colophon

Acknowledgements

LIQUIFER are thankful to everyone who has worked with the team over the years. Valentin Eder, a co-managing director and designer was crucial to the development of the practice from 2011-2014. Petra Gruber was a pivotal co-lead in the GRaB project. We also want to thank (in alphabetical order): Olisa Agulue, Anna Balint, Darren Berlein, Irmgard Derschmidt, Norbert Frischauf, Sandra Häuplik-Meusburger, Kjell Herrmann, Molly Hogle-Stiefel, Melanie Klähn, Barbara Kolb, Sonia Leimer, Ewa Lenart, Paul Mayr, Damjan Minovski, Kürsad Özdemir, Georg Pamperl, Wolfgang Prohaska, Lutz Richter, Anne-Marlene Ruede, Nina Soltani, Anna Stürzenbecher, Angelo Vermeulen and Kaspar Vogel. With his permission LIQUIFER has used 3D models from Swiss artist Max Grüter for their visualisations. We are extremely grateful to those without whom this book wouldn't have been possible: the team at PARK Books who supported our vision, friends who gave feedback early in the development of the book, Matthew Ponsford for his deft editing skills and of course to designers Nik Thoenen and Hannah Sakai.

In memoriam of Bob Davenport.

Imprint

Concept:
Jennifer Cunningham & LIQUIFER
Authors:
Jennifer Cunningham, Waltraut Hoheneder, Barbara Imhof, René Waclavicek, Brent Sherwood and Christina Ciardullo
Copy editing:
Matthew Ponsford
Proofreading:
Jennifer Cunningham, Waltraut Hoheneder and Barbara Imhof

Design:
Nik Thoenen, Hannah Sakai
Image processing:
Pascal Petignat, Nik Thoenen
Paper:
Lahnur, Multicolor Mirabell, Lona Art
Typefaces:
MicroNova, Lexik
Printing and binding:
Gugler GmbH

© 2023 LIQUIFER and Park Books AG, Zurich

© for the texts: the authors
© for the images: the artists / see image credits

Park Books
Niederdorfstrasse 54
8001 Zurich
Switzerland
www.park-books.com

Park Books is being supported by the Federal Office of Culture with a general subsidy for the years 2021–2024.

All rights reserved; no part of this publication may be reproduced, stored in a retrieval system or transmitted in any form or by any means, electronic, mechanical, photocopying, recording, or otherwise, without the prior written consent of the publisher.

ISBN 978-3-03860-345-0

Federal Ministry
Republic of Austria
Arts, Culture,
Civil Service and Sport